Wise as an Owl
and
Sly as a Fox

by

Loice Kendrick-Lacy

FOREWORD

As a life member of the Arkansas Audubon Society, I wrote nature articles for many years for each issue of the quarterly newsletter. In this book, I will use much of the information I included in those articles. However, revisions will be necessary as much has changed in the world of plants and animals since my last article was published over 30 years ago.

DEDICATION

This book is dedicated to all lovers of nature the world over. No matter the season, no matter the location, Mother Nature always has something we can enjoy.

ACKNOWLEDGEMENTS

I appreciate all who have shared information with me for this book, as well as the many who have furnished the photographs for it. The names of the photographers, the titles of their submissions and the page numbers on which they appear will be listed at the end of the book text.

CONTENTS

WISE AS AN OWL

The expression "wise as an owl" can be traced back to Greek mythology. The Goddess of Wisdom, Athena, was often represented as an owl. In Hindu mythology an owl is seen as the vehicle of the Goddess of Wealth, Lakshmi. Often this wealth was gained by foul means and thus the owl was considered a symbol of foolishness. The wise owl appears in everything from the Iliad to Winnie the Pooh.

I like this poem by Edward Richards Hersey:

> A wise old owl sat in an oak.
> The more he saw, the less he spoke.
> The less he spoke, the more he heard.
> Why can't we be like this wise old bird?

There are 18 species of owls that appear in the United States. They range in length from the twenty-two-inch great gray owl to the elf owl, which is only five and one-fourth inches long. Some people believe that owls can turn their heads completely around, but they can only turn them 270 degrees in either direction. What makes this possible is that owls have twice as many vertebrae in their necks as we do. An owl's eyes are fixed in their sockets so the entire head must be turned to shift their gaze.

Most owls are active at night and find a sheltered spot to rest during the day. The velvety surface and soft edges of owl feathers are not as water repellent as typical feathers, so owls tend to get wet in the rain. They seek out sheltered daytime roost sites in hollow trees or dense vegetation. Sometimes other birds or squirrels discover a roosting owl and mob it.

Barred owls are common in swamps and river bottoms, but less common, although widespread in northern woods. They measure 17 inches in length and are one of the five species of our owls with dark eyes. They nest in cavities or in the old nest of a large bird such as a hawk. They even use the old nests of squirrels sometimes.

They are usually single-brooded, but will replace a lost clutch. Breeding begins in mid-January in the south and mid-March in the north. The eggs are white and a clutch usually consists of 2 to 3, but may be as many as 4. Incubation is by the female, but both parents attend the young.

Boreal owls are found in the Far North coming into the northern United States in the winter. They are 10 inches in length and have yellow eyes. Being mostly nocturnal, only in the arctic summer do they feed by day. Their calls are a series of whistles that sound like dripping water.

This owl breeds in woodlands, usually in cavities in conifers, old holes of woodpeckers or even in constructed nest boxes. Breeding begins mid-April and commonly single-brooded, but occasionally double-brooded. The eggs are white and a clutch usually consists of 3 to 6 but may be as many as 10 when food is plentiful. The female does all the incubation and tending to the young. Where's that lazy male parent?

The "horns" on the top of the head of a great horned owl are actually tufts of feathers that can be raised or lowered according to the owl's mood.

GREAT HORNED OWL

The great horned owl is one of our largest, measuring 20 inches in length. It is the most widespread of all our owls, being found in every state and province of North America. This owl can be found in many towns, feeding on the abundance of small mammals found there. You might say it takes the night shift, whereas hawks are on the day shift. The great horned owl's call is typically four to seven low hoots.

These owls breed in a wide range of woodland habitat. They nest in a natural tree, in a fork of a giant cactus, on a rock ledge, and often in the old nest of a large bird in such sites. Breeding begins in late November to January in the south and April in the north. They are usually single brooded but may replace a lost clutch. A clutch of the white eggs is most often 2 to 3, but can be as many as 5. Incubation is by female alone, but both parents tend the young.

A burrowing owl is a long-legged diurnal owl of the plains. It has yellow eyes and is only 8 inches in length. In Florida, these owls inhabit prairies and airports. The daytime calls are a cackling alarm note and at night they utter a coo-c-o-o. They have a habit of bobbing up and down with a quick bending motion of the legs.

Writing this about the owl's bobbing motion reminds me of something a student at the Arkansas Audubon Ecology camp told me one year when I was there as an Ornithology instructor. He was asking me what kind of bird was the one he was seeing near the water's edge. I was having a problem spotting the bird so I asked him what the bird was doing. He answered, "He's doing pushups." I knew immediately that it was a waterthrush and showed him its picture in my field guide. He agreed that was the bird he was seeing.

Burrowing owls are single-brooded unless a clutch needs replacing. The breeding season begins in late March in the south and early May in the north. They nest in burrows of ground squirrels, badgers, and tortoises, enlarging them if necessary. Nest chambers are lined with such things as cow dung, stalks, feathers, grasses, bones and any rubbish available. (Garbage collectors?). These appear to be our only owls bringing materials into a cavity. The white eggs are usually laid in a clutch of 5 to 6 but may be as many as 11.

Elf owls are the smallest of our owls, being only five and one-fourth inches in length. They are nocturnal and common in southwestern deserts. They are best seen at dusk in saguaro deserts, as they roost during the day in holes in this giant cactus. Call is a rapid high-pitched series of six or more cackling notes.

The elf owl breeds in desert regions, usually in an old woodpecker nest in a giant cactus or a tree. Breeding season begins in early May. A clutch of the white eggs usually consists of three, but sometimes two to five. Both parents share in incubation and tending the young.

Ferruginous owls are uncommon and found in wooded river bottoms and saguaro deserts in the southern parts of Arizona and Texas near the Mexican border. They are only 6 inches in length and have yellow eyes. Their call is a long series of single notes. They call during the day, but more frequently at night.

Ferruginous owls nest in old woodpecker holes or in tree cavities. The eggs are white and laid in a clutch of 3 to 4. These owls often feed during the day and are sometimes mobbed by other birds.

Flammulated owls measure 6 inches in length and are our only small owl with dark eyes. They are rare and local in the extreme western United States. Their call is a long repetition of single or double low-pitched hoots repeated for long periods at a rate of 40 to 60 per minute.

These owls' nest in old woodpecker holes or tree cavities in montane pine woods. They are single-brooded with breeding season beginning in mid-May to early June. The 3 to 4 eggs in a clutch are white and slightly glossy.

Great gray owls are our largest owls measuring 22 inches in length and have yellow eyes. They are rare and local at high elevations in north and central Sierra Nevada and Rockies. Their call is a deep booming series of whos, each lower in pitch.

They breed in conifer forests on the top of broken off tree trunks or in the old nests of other large birds. They are single-brooded and the breeding season begins in late March. They may not nest at all in unfavorable years. The white eggs are usually laid in clutches of 3 to 5, but sometimes fewer and in good years may be as many as 9. Incubation is by female alone and she feeds the young on food brought by the male.

A hawk owl is 14 inches in length and has yellow eyes. It has a long slender tail that gives it a falcon-like appearance, thus the name hawk owl. It perches in the open on tree tops where it has a habit of raising its tail and then slowly lowering it. Sometimes it sits with its tail cocked up at an angle. Its call is a series of whistles uttered at 10 to 15 groups each minute.

The hawk owl nests in conifer and birch forests. The breeding season begins in April to early May. It nests in tree cavities, old woodpecker holes, hollows at ends of broken tree trunks, and old nests of other large birds. Usually single-brooded, but sometimes two in good food years. The eggs are glossy white and usually laid in a clutch of 3 to 10, but rarely as many as 13, depending on food supply. Most incubation done by female, but the male sometimes gives her a break. Both parents tend the young. Hooray for that male!

Long-eared owls are locally common in deciduous or coniferous woods near open country. They are 13 inches in length and have yellow eyes. They are generally silent except near their nests where they make a variety of low hoots, whistles and shrieks.

They frequently use old nests of another bird or squirrel, but more rarely the nest is on the ground sheltered by the base of a tree or among low shrubs. Breeding begins in early March in the south and mid-April in the north. Usually single-brooded but may be double in good food years. The glossy white eggs are usually laid in a clutch of 4 or 5, rarely 3 to 8. Incubation is generally by female alone and the young are fed with food brought by the male. Another good guy!

A pygmy owl is only 6 inches in length, has yellow eyes and a long tail that is usually cocked at an angle. It is a common, tame owl of coniferous and deciduous woods. Its call is a long repetition of single or double dove-like notes uttered at 60 to 80 per minute.

It breeds in forests, placing its nest in a natural tree cavity or an old woodpecker hole in a tree. It is single-brooded, with the breeding season beginning in late April or early May. A clutch usually contains 4 to 6 eggs, but sometimes 3 to 7. They are white and slightly glossy. Incubation is by female and she broods the young. She feeds them on food brought by the male.

Saw whet owls measure 7 inches in length, have yellow eyes and a very short tail. They are nocturnal and more common than often thought to be because they are seldom seen unless spotted roosting in dense young evergreens or in thickets. Their call is a long series of short whistles.

They breed in woodlands, often in swampy areas. They nest in old woodpecker holes and less often in natural tree cavities. The breeding season begins in mid-March to mid-April. The eggs in a clutch are usually 5 to 6, but sometimes 4 to 7. The eggs are white, smooth and sometimes, but not always, slightly glossy. Incubation is by the female.

Barn owls and at least four other species of owls have one ear pointing upward and the other pointing down. This enables them to hear sounds better from both above and below. Owls have extremely sensitive hearing, but most owls still require some vision to capture prey. However, barn owls can capture prey in total darkness by sound. A test proved that a barn owl located a mouse 30 feet away by the sound the rodent made.

BARN OWLS

The barn owl is 14 inches in length, has small dark eyes and long legs. It is strictly nocturnal, hunting rats and mice on which to feed. This owl does not hoot, but has an ascending wheezy cry. At the nest it gives a toneless hiss. It nests in barns, abandoned buildings and tree cavities. Their breeding season begins in January in the south and February to early March in the north. Often double-brooded, a clutch is usually 4 to 7 eggs, but occasionally may contain as many as 11. The eggs are white and incubated by female alone with the male bringing her food. Both parents tend and feed the young.

A screech owl is active at night and finds a secluded spot to rest during the day. It is a common small "eared" owl of towns, orchards and small woodlots. It measures 8 inches in length and has yellow eyes. Its call is a series of quavering whistles, sometimes monotone and descending.

Its breeding season begins early March in the south and mid-April in the north. The nest may be in a natural tree cavity, in an old woodpecker hole, including those in telegraph poles and cacti in some areas. A clutch of eggs is usually 4 to 5 but sometimes 3 to 7. The eggs are white, smooth and slightly glossy. Both incubation and brooding of the young is done by the female, with the male bringing her food during incubation and to both her and the young during brooding.

Short-eared owls are 13 inches in length and have yellow eyes. The ears are hard to see as they are so short. Their wings are tilted upward. These owls are active before dark and are usually silent.

These owls breed in open country, on plains, prairies, marshes or dunes. Their nests are on the ground, sheltered by tall grass, reeds or bushes. The breeding season usually begins in late April but sometimes two or three weeks earlier. They are usually single-brooded but may be double when food is plentiful. A clutch usually consists of 4 to 8, but again when food is plentiful, there may be up to 14 laid. The eggs are white, smooth, and may be either non-glossy or slightly glossy. Incubation and brooding of the young is by the female, with the male bringing food for her during incubation and later for both her and the young.

Snowy owls are 20 inches in length, have dark eyes and the adults are almost snow white. This is an owl of the arctic region that winters irregularly in the northern United States. It perches near the ground in open country and will allow birders to get very close to it. It is silent south of its breeding ground. It feeds on lemmings, other rodents and rabbits.

Although it doesn't breed in the United States, I will cover its nesting information here. It breeds in level open country, on arctic tundra, on islands or mountains. Its nest may be on the ground, but sometimes on a large boulder or crag. It is single-brooded and may not nest at all in some years. Breeding begins late May to early June. A clutch varies with food supply, usually 4 to 10, but sometimes as many as 15. The eggs are white, smooth and slightly glossy. Incubation and brooding is by the female with the male bringing food during both cycles.

A spotted owl is 16 inches in length, has dark eyes, a short tail and, as the name indicates, has clusters of spots on its sides, back and head. It is found in the far western United States. Its call consists of three or four hoots.

It breeds in conifer forests and forested canyons. It is single-brooded and the nesting season begins in early March. The eggs are white, smooth and slightly glossy. Nest may be in a natural cavity in a tree, more rarely in the old nest of a large bird in a tree or cave, and sometimes in a cave or on a rocky slope.

A whiskered owl is six and one-half inches in length, has a short tail and yellow eyes. And guess what? It appears to have forgotten to shave. In the United States it is found only in southeastern Arizona where it is common. It is found in canyons, generally in dense oak or oak-pine woods. Its distinctive call is a series of 4 to 9 high-pitched boos, vaguely suggestive of a white-winged dove.

This owl nests in a tree cavity or an old woodpecker hole. Its breeding season begins in early May. The eggs are white, smooth and slightly glossy. A clutch usually consists of three eggs, but sometimes 4 are laid.

Night owl prowls are popular with birders. Many of the birders are so adept with imitating an owl's call that they can get owls to respond and come to perch in a tree near the birders. They then shine a light up into the tree for all to view them. Personally, I have to use recorded calls as my uttered calls never get any results.

WOODPECKERS: SURVIVAL OF THE FITTEST

We have 23 species of woodpeckers in the United States. 18 have woodpecker in their names, 3 are called flickers and 2 are called sapsuckers. Woodpeckers are a family of forest-dwelling birds that have acquired individual specializations in competition for their own good and are endangered or extinct, while others sustain or increase their populations by continuing to adapt to changing environments. All woodpeckers nest in holes bored in trees. Similar holes may be bored outside of breeding season to roost in. The eggs are white, smooth and rounded. The young are fed mostly on food regurgitated by the parent birds.

Extensive alteration of the habitat of woodpeckers of North America began as the pioneers cleared land for agriculture and continues with today's lumbering practices. The total acreage in forests as a whole in North America has decreased by 30 to 40 percent since pre-Columbian times.

Even species within a genus that appear to be comparable and are found in the same habitat may respond differently to a change in their surroundings because they occupy their own special niche in their community. To illustrate how similar birds sometimes react in widely diverse ways to habitat disturbance, six woodpeckers have been selected, two of each of two genera and two others sharing a number of characteristics one with the other.

IVORY-BILLED WOODPECKER

The birds considered are grouped in three pairs. Of these, probably the pileated and the ivory-billed woodpeckers offer the most extreme contrast in population changes due to habitat destruction. Our largest woodpeckers are the

11

ivory-billed measuring 20 inches in length and the pileated 18 inches. The birds look enough alike to confuse many people. To distinguish between the two, note the ivory color of the beak of ivory-billed and the dark bill of the pileated. The ivory-billed has extensive white wing patches while the pileated has a black back.

Although both woodpeckers once had a wide range throughout eastern virgin forests, with the logging of those forests, the pileated has been able to adapt to changing conditions while the ivory-billed was declared extinct in September of 2021. There may still be some ivory-billed woodpeckers in the pine forests of eastern Cuba.

In spite of their similarities, the pileated woodpecker occupies a far broader ecological niche than that of the highly specialized ivory-billed. The limitations of its diet is one of the reasons for the downfall of the ivory-billed. It fed primarily on larvae of a group of bark beetles found solely in aged, often dead, trees. With timber cutting that eliminated the mature forests, the ivory-billed was doomed.

Pileated Woodpecker

A male Pileated Woodpecker

PILEATED WOODPECKER

Although the pileated eats those bark beetles, it has a varied diet that includes other insects as well as the fruits of various trees, shrubs and vines. Seventy percent of its diet is animal matter with more that half being ants of various kinds. Included in the thirty percent of plant food are the fruits of oak, wild cherry, Virginia creeper, elderberry, holly, grape, blackgum, sassafras, buckthorn and dogwood.

Man's encroachment destroyed the ivory-billed, but the pileated, although it declined when the mature forests were first cleared, has become more abundant in this century. It is now seen in towns and around farmhouses as well as in heavily wooded areas. Once my sister-in-law who lived across the street from me, called me to come see a pileated woodpecker working the trunk of a large live oak tree. Unmindful of the traffic not 20 feet away, he hammered away for at least ten minutes seemingly intent on felling the tree.

The second pair of woodpeckers to be compared are the downy and red-cockaded. The downy is the smallest of our woodpeckers, measuring only five and three-fourths inches in length, while the red-cockaded is slightly longer at seven and one-fourth. The downy is abundant all over the United States while the red-cockaded is in deep trouble. Diet does not seem to play a role in the decline of the red-cockaded as it feeds on many kinds of insects and the fruits of numerous species of wild plants. It is the need of a very selective nesting and foraging area that limits the red-cockaded.

Early in the nineteenth century, John James Audubon wrote of the abundance of the red-cockaded woodpecker, but populations have severely decreased with the loss of highly specialized habitat. For nesting, these birds must have aged living pine trees at least 60 years old infected with red heart rot. The red-cockaded was placed on the Endangered Species List in 1973. So many of the nesting sites are in forest lands owned by the private timber industry. Private industry is not obligated to protect endangered species.

The final two species used to illustrate how forest-dwelling birds have responded to habitat alteration are the red-bellied and the red-headed woodpeckers. The red-headed woodpecker has declined in numbers because of loss of nesting sites. Man not only reduced the number of available sites through the cutting of timber and snags, he introduced starlings brought from Europe to New York in 1890.

The relatively meek red-headed will allow the aggressive starling to utilize all suitable sites. The woodpecker may excavate cavity after cavity only to have them taken over by the encroaching starling. The red-bellied shares much of the same range of the red-headed, but not the fate. Both species frequently haunt backyards, orchards and scattered groves of deciduous trees. The two excavate their nesting holes in dead wood of a variety of trees, in telephone poles or fence posts. It is here the similarity between the two woodpeckers ends. While the red-headed will yield to intruders like the starling, the red-bellied will battle for hours if necessary to protect his territory against invaders. Thus the populations of the red-headed declined, while the red-bellied is now the most abundant woodpecker in part of its range.

In 1977 the United States Forest Service established a national snag policy to develop guidelines to provide habitat needed to maintain viable, self-sustaining populations of cavity-nesting and snag-dependent wildlife species. The scope of the policy includes retention of selected trees, snags, and other flora to meet future habitat requirements. Such policies can mean brighter futures for some cavity-nesters, but came too late to save the ivory-billed woodpecker and aid the endangered red-cockaded.

HUNGRY AS A HERON

The great blue heron who never seems to be in a hurry when flying, stalking his prey or merely sitting tirelessly watching the water's surface for food, can move with paradoxical swiftness when spearing a fish. The water is scarcely disturbed as he cautiously lifts a partially-webbed foot above the surface and quietly eases it forward and down. Long, widely-spaced toes keep him from sinking too far into the muck. All is slow motion until a fish swims by and the spear-like bill, powered by long neck muscles. shoots forward to lance the prey.

A small fish is tossed in the air by the heron and caught to be swallowed head first so that the fins flatten against the body of the fish as it slides down the bird's narrow elongated neck. If the fish is large, the heron may go ashore to beat it against a hard surface to render it palatable.

The great blue heron, largest member of the heron family in North America, has a life span of about 15 years of which most of the time may be spent in a concentrated area. However, bird banding projects and recoveries in Texas show that some birds banded there in the winter have migrated from as far away as Montana, Wyoming, Washington, Nebraska, Illinois, Wisconsin, and Alberta and Saskatchewan in Canada.

Great blue herons stand about four feet high when the head is raised. They are blue-gray in color with white on the head, black slash marks over the eyes, and plumes on back and breast. Often miscalled "cranes", the great blues can easily be distinguished from their cousins by flight posture. Although both fly with long legs trailing behind, the heron pulls its neck back on its shoulders in an S-shaped curve while cranes fly with outstretched necks. The broad, rounded wings of the great blue heron have a span of over six feet in flight.

GREAT BLUE HERON

With stilt-like legs for wading knee deep in the shallows and a long compensating neck that can up periscope above tall marsh grasses, the great blue makes its living catching fish, crustaceans, amphibians, insects and a few small mammals. Because of their fish-eating habits, they have been widely persecuted by fishermen, However, the majority of fish they eat are enemies of man.

In order to satisfy his ravenous appetite, the great blue heron feeds almost constantly during the day, a habit which generated the expression "hungry as a heron." In contrast, the common egret, which is similar in muscular structure and many habits, feeds far less often.

Loners for most of the year, great blues form colonies of mated pairs during the breeding season. They nest by either fresh or salt water, building their flat platform nests of weeds and twigs in trees, on rocky cliffs, or duck blinds. Thin and small when newly built, the nests may be added to yearly, becoming quite bulky. The greenish-blue eggs may number from three to seven, commonly four.

Both parents share in the building of the nest, incubation and feeding the young. The adults bring food in the crop and are induced to disgorge it when the baby seizes the bill of the parent bird in its own. At first, regurgitation is late-stage, but later whole prey may be regurgitated.

The great blue sitting on the fishing pier gazing at the water's surface or perched atop a snag with head hunched on shoulders is not idling away his time. He is exhibiting true heron perseverance in his endless quest for food. If in spite of his patience, the waters prove unproductive, he will lift with heavy wings and fly with slow, measured gait to another site seeking to sate his voracious appetite.

AVIAN ARCHITECTURE

Any receptacle for the deposit of eggs is called a nest. Although most birds build some type of nest, a number of waterfowl and a few land birds lay eggs on bare ground, rock or other objects. For example, auks and murres deposit a single egg on ledges or rock; common nighthawks lay their eggs on bare earth or graveled roofs of buildings; and fairy terns place their single egg on a tree branch to which the hatchling is capable of clinging immediately after emerging from the shell.

Among some bird species both the male and female share in building the nest and among others the female alone performs the task. In the unusual case of our native phalaropes, the male takes complete responsibility for building the nest, incubating the eggs and caring for the young. In complete role reversal, the liberated females even wear the brighter plumage and take the initiative in courtship.

CARDINAL NEST WITH BABIES

The type of nest needed is largely determined by the degree of dependence of the young when hatched. Generally, species most at home on the ground or in the water, such as loons, grebes, cranes, coots, rails, ducks, geese and other shorebirds lay relatively large eggs in relation to the size of the female. The young are hatched open-eyed, covered with down, and capable of scampering or paddling about almost at once. Birds of this type are called precocial and need little in the way of a nest. Birds that are most at home perching, such as herons, falcons and other hawks, doves, pigeons, owls, hummingbirds, swifts, and woodpeckers lay relatively small eggs. Their altricial young are hatched blind, naked, able only to lie prostate and beg open-mouthed for food. For these birds a more elaborate nest is needed.

Nest types are extremely diversified among birds, but vary little within a species. Of the cup-shaped nests which are the most common form, those of the tiny hummingbirds rank high for intricacy in avian architecture. Constructed of fine plant material, the nests are bound together and anchored in place with spider webs. The lichen covering the exterior of the nest blends them into the supporting branch of a tree.

Orioles are among the master builders with their long pendulous nests. Those of the giant orioles of Central America, woven of grasses and palm leaves, are almost six feet long. Our northern oriole begins her swinging cradle with pieces of string which she fastens to the tip of a bough, leaving the ends dangling. She then weaves in various materials to complete a sack about six inches long.

Using stitch work of the kind physicians call suturing, the tailorbird of southern Asia sews the edges of a large leaf to another one to form a receptacle for its nest. It punctures the margins of the leaves with holes and stitches the edges together with thread of plant fiber, insect silk or spider webs. If necessary, the bird even knots the thread to secure the ends.

Unique among nests is the large communal structure made by the social weavers of South Africa. A few to over 100 individuals working together construct a huge mass of dried grass placed several feet above the ground in a tree. Each pair makes its nesting hole in the massive condominium which may reach a height of ten or more feet.

An unusual type of ground nest is that built by megapodes of the Australian region. They scrape together a large mound of rotting vegetable matter in which they lay their eggs, leaving them to be incubated by the heat generated by the decomposition of the vegetation. One such mound measured 15 feet wide, 10 feet high and 60 feet long. Many of us could learn the value of composting from these birds.

WOOD DUCK NEST WITH EGGS

Numerous species of birds, some 65 in North America alone, are cavity nesters. They excavate nesting sites in trees or posts, utilize holes made by other species, use cavities created by decay, or nest in bird houses. Remarkable among the cavity nesters are the horn bills. As soon as the female has begun incubation of the eggs, the male imprisons her by plastering the tree hole with mud, leaving only a small aperture through which he feeds her and later the young. The hatchlings develop safe from predation in their sealed prison until old enough to fend for themselves. The male then breaks away the plaster to release his family.

The majority of nests are built of such things as sticks, twigs, rootlets, weed stems, grasses and lichens, and lined with softer materials like hair, cotton, wool and plant down. The principal material used by many species of swallows is mud, while most phoebes and thrushes use some mud in conjunction with plant fibers.

Chimney swifts use their saliva to cement their nests together and the surface to which they are attached. Some swift nests are made entirely of coagulated saliva. The Chinese use the nests of certain swifts native to Southeastern Asia as the principal ingredient for bird's nest soup, a luxury food. Hungry, anyone? A profitable business is made by leasing the nesting caves and selling the nests which have the appearance of milky isinglass. Granted the soup may be a gourmet's delight, the virtual appeal of the glutinous mass is such that the first potful must have been happenstance. My theory is that a nest must have become unglued from the cave wall and fell into an early-age Oriental soup pot simmering over an open fire.

The tiny palm swift, which breeds from Africa eastward to the Pacific, cements a concave pad of down and feathers together on a palm leaf. The eggs are glued in with the bird's mucilaginous saliva to keep them from falling out. The adults cling to the vertical pad to incubate the eggs, and the young are able likewise to keep a secure grip from the moment of hatching.

Nests are as variable in size as they are in type of architecture. While size is not always directly related to that of the builder, the tiniest of all nests is a cup not much larger than a thimble built by the smallest of birds, the bee hummingbird of Cuba. In contrast are the massive structures of bald eagles, which are added to year after year. One nest used for 34 years was estimated to weigh over two tons and be 20 feet deep by 9 ½ feet across.

Most ornithologists agree that birds are not cunning enough to hide their nests deliberately, but that concealment results from the type of surroundings preferred by the species. Be that as it may, when the leaves are stripped from the trees in the fall revealing all those nests you knew were there but never could find, you will want to attribute a high degree of intelligence to the master builders who have again outsmarted you.

BAHAMA BIRDING ON THE SLY

The signs one sees everywhere in the Bahamas Islands proclaiming "It's better in the Bahamas" could be applied to some birding experiences I had there in very early April one year. While one cannot expect to see an impressive number of species on the islands, it was the quality of birding that was laudable. For instance, a green heron, a species that usually departs with a voiced loud skeow whenever I get near, lingered to pose for photographs at a distance of about six feet and a Swainson's warbler was so sociable that eventually I was the one who left, not the warbler.

However, in order to have any notable birding encounters during my stay in the Bahamas, I had needed all the help from the birds I could get. I was on the islands as a member of a group of ten, nine of which would scarcely have known a woodstar from a woodpecker. When my husband Cecil and I were invited to join his sisters and brothers and their spouses for a week in the Bahamas, I knew I would have to sneak in my birding as best I could. Realizing I would likely become obsessed with the birds in an unfamiliar territory, Cecil had made me promise not to hamper any group plans by indulging my hobby. I anticipated a pleasurable week engaged in activities comparable with the interests of the others, with a little birding on the sly.

We arrived on New Providence Island in mid-afternoon, On the trip from the airport through the country to South Ocean Beach Hotel, we rode for several minutes before I spotted my first bird. Initially I thought the mockingbird singing atop a post beside the road presented a familiar sight. Just as I got close enough to view the bird's brownish coloration and striping along the flanks, the singer lifted from its perch and flew parallel to the car. No white wing patches were visible. A Bahama mockingbird! My first life bird for the trip and I had added it with so little effort.

As we got out of the car in front of our hotel, a flock of palm warblers were feeding beneath the shrubbery, constantly flirting their tails in a characteristic manner. The tame little ground-feeders would prove to be one of the most abundant species I saw during the week. I encountered natives who called these birds "chip-chips", a local name for many small warblers.

Carefully packed among my luggage was a hummingbird feeder and a container of sweetened water. Surely I could add the Bahama woodstar to my life list simply by enticing them to feed outside my hotel window. But alas! There was no place to hang the feeder outside the room assigned to us. Reminding myself that if I were going to succeed at my little game of sneaky birding, I was going to have to keep on my toes, so I hung the feeder by a brother-in-law's window.

The Bahama woodstar is said to be the only hummingbird native to the Bahamas, however there are old records of a ruby-throat and an emerald appearing on New Providence. Although the woodstar is said to be abundant in the Bahamas, I never saw one at my feeder nor any evidence that any birds had fed there. Perhaps woodstars don't frequent feeders. I saw feeders for other birds on the islands but none for hummers, but that doesn't preclude their being there.

Unpacking completed, the others pleaded jet lag and opted to stay in their rooms for awhile. With a clear conscience I grabbed my binoculars and hastened outside. South Beach Hotel is a golf resort in the country at the southwest tip of New Providence. Although the grounds offer an array of blooms on bedding plants, shrubs and trees, I was disappointed that I couldn't spot even one woodstar.

I headed toward the 600 foot private beach a few hundred yards away where a volleyball game was in progress. Tame little ground doves were all but being stepped on by the players. Cooing monotonously and nodding their scaled heads as they walked, the small doves were everywhere on the ground and in the casuarinas and coconut palms. Down the beach west of the volleyball court was a flock of beachcombers: black-bellied plovers, the jet-black of their breeding plumage beginning to show on the underparts; semipalmated plovers; short-billed dowitchers; and ruddy turnstones turning stones and bits of flotsam in search of food. Two royal terns were fishing just offshore flying in formation low over the water.

Moving slightly inland I spotted a hairy woodpecker drumming against the trunk of a casuarina. This was the only woodpecker I saw in the Bahamas, indeed the only one I expected to see in New Providence at this time of year. As I walked along the outer edge of the coppice and scrub, I heard many birds singing. One that sounded like the white-eyed vireo proved to be the thick-billed species, a bird I spotted on a low limb carrying nesting material in its mouth. The constant song of this vireo was to be as much a part of every trip afield on the islands as that of the white-eyed is on field trips during the breeding season in the southeastern United States.

BANANAQUIT

I was hearing another song which I didn't recognize but shortly paired with the singer, a black-faced grassquit, an abundant resident of the Bahamas. Later in the week I added a second member of the Tiaris genus to my life list, the melodious grassquit. About 300 birds of this species were released on New Providence in March of 1963 when a plane carrying a consignment of birds from Cuba to a zoo in Europe made an emergency landing in Nassau. After many of the birds had died because of the unexpected delay, the rest were freed. Both the melodious and a few yellow-faced grassquits released at the time of the emergency landing have established populations on New Providence, but I was not fortunate enough to see any of the latter species.

Late in the day just before dusk, having changed quickly and waiting for the others to get dressed for dinner, I pulled my hiking boots back on and slipped out the back door of the hotel. Sneaky, sneaky. It was darker than I had thought, so I didn't see any birds, but while passing near some tall trees at the edge of the golf course, I heard flapping of wings as a startled flock roosting there moved further into the woods. They sounded like large birds and it was with eager anticipation I determined to check them out the next morning.

Early morning was my bonus time for birding, All the others slept late so by getting out by six, I was guaranteed at least two hours of birding before getting back to the hotel to prepare for whatever was planned for the day. While vainly searching for Bahama woodstars around the hotel early that first morning, I encountered a friendly native working the flower beds. We chatted for a few minutes about the plants and birds around us. To my query as to why I was not seeing any hummingbirds among so many blossoms, he first looked puzzled, then said, "Hummingbirds? Oh, you mean those little guys. . ." here his voice trailed off as he beat his arms rapidly against his sides. On being assured those were the little guys in question, he added, "It's too cold for them now. Come back about 9:00 and they should be out". It was nearly 70 degrees at the time, hardly a temperature to inhibit a hummingbird, I thought. But I thanked him politely; whatever he might lack in bird knowledge he made up for in genial disposition.

Heading around behind the hotel I noticed several large birds perched atop the trees. Even without magnification I could see some of the birds had glistening white heads. I was so excited about adding the white-crowned pigeon to my life list that I must have stood there several minutes viewing their field marks before I realized these were the large birds that clattered through the trees the night before.

I planned to walk around the golf course staying close to the trees so that I could pick up birds of both habitats. Shortly I sighted a merlin flying low over the open ground. It was to be my only listing for the week of an essentially aerial bird other than the terns and laughing gulls that patrolled Nassau Harbor. My attention was quickly diverted from the merlin by a loud repetitive "wheep". I recognized the call as that of a stolid flycatcher by reason of the homework I had done on bird song before I left home. Actually, I had not studied as much as I should have because I was not going to be birding, was I? The wheeper cinched the identification as the flycatcher sallied forth to grab an insect on the wing and return to perch high in a tree.

Numerous warbler species were seen all around the perimeter of the golf course: black and white, northern parula, yellow-rumped, pine, magnolia, prairie, palm, and Cape May. Second in abundance to the palm warblers seemed to be the Cape Mays, which in some spots studded the trees like Christmas tree ornaments. Their performance was gratifying as prior to this trip my encounters with them had been less than satisfactory. In fact, in all my efforts to view warblers, never have I found them as cooperative as in the Bahamas.

Along my route I sighted a pair of bobwhites, a common snipe and several black-faced grassquits before seeing my next new species, a greater antillian pewee. It was neither singing nor feeding, just posing on a low branch for me to check off his field marks. Time to head back to the hotel and I had not covered half the distance around the golf course. I retraced my steps with plans to bird the other side the next morning.

A car was coming shortly to take us to Ardastra Gardens. About 15 minutes before the car was to arrive, I was back out front of the hotel when I located a female woodstar hummingbird just as the gardener had promised. She sat on a low shrub affording me a good view but my first woodstar didn't get the attention she deserved as I felt compelled to make a quick, but vain, search for a male. A couple of other hummingbirds flitting around the blooming hibiscus were also females.

Ardastra Gardens is in the country just west of Nassau and contains a number of small ponds where exotic species mingle with a few natives. Greater flamingoes marching in formation are featured in a show presented twice daily. Although they are the national bird of the Bahamas, captive flamingoes such as these are all you will see on New Providence. A very large breeding colony does exist in the wild on Great Inagua with possibly smaller ones on Abaco and Andros.

Many things touted in the brochure for Ardastra Gardens were a disappointment to me, but what I didn't read in the ads was that a Greater Antillean bullfinch would be perched quietly beneath an arbor built over a garden path, nor that bananaquits would be flitting everywhere among the flowers. Although these birds favor much the same diet as hummingbirds, they cannot hover like the hummers and must cling in some acrobatic manner to the plant while feeding. I spent much time at Ardastra amused by these darling little yellow-rumped gymnasts.

During my second morning walk around the golf course I saw many of the species of the previous day with the addition of two prizes. The first was a great lizard cuckoo I located after hearing rustling in the undergrowth. Its size is close to that of a roadrunner and indeed it is like the roadrunner in other ways as well. It runs more than it flies and it feeds on insects and lizards. My second new bird for the day was a stripe-headed tanager which revealed his presence by his call which I didn't recognize although I had been hearing it all along my route. Either there was more than one tanager or the bird was moving with me. Singing accompaniment to the tanager were several indigo buntings who brightened the morning with their song and flashes of brilliant blue.

Then it was time to return to the hotel and I had not covered even as long a distance as the previous morning. And alas! This was to be my last day to bird this area as we were moving to the Pilot House, a hotel in Nassau. The move was for the convenience of the others of our group who wanted to be closer in as transportation from South Ocean Beach was both expensive and time-consuming.

The Pilot House had more than its share of ringed turtle doves, an Old World species. Other than the doves, I saw no other birds on the hotel grounds except mockingbirds in the parking area. Still I found some good places for my early morning field trips simply by walking a short distance to an unpopulated district.

RED-LEGGED THRUSH

On a boat trip we took one day we docked at the east end of Paradise Island for a short time ashore. While the others of our party walked the sandy beach, I headed inland along a trail through the dense coppice and scrub. I shared the trail with an abundance of lizards and one friendly snake. (There are no poisonous snakes in the Bahamas). I saw no birds although they kept up a constant chatter in the jungle-like vegetation. Shortly the trail intersected a small stream bed. I had read that there were no streams in the islands except Andros, but call it what you will, this was a long low area cut through the terrain with water standing here and there. And the habitat produced such stream-side birds as a common yellowthroat and several very tame northern waterthrushes. A narrow wooded area separated the streambed from the Paradise Golf Course. On the ground and in the trees adjoining the course I counted eight smooth-billed anis, a species I'd never seen before. It was my custom to ask natives the local names of the birds I was seeing. More often than not, the natives could not supply a name, but in the case of the anis, a native on the golf course said, "Those are just old crows."

Another day, Cecil and one of his brothers and I took a Robinson Crusoe cruise to Rose Island, a very tiny island to the north of Lake Providence and Paradise Island. We were to spend several hours there snorkeling and enjoying a picnic lunch cooked over an open fire, while the others of our party had chosen to go to the Sea Gardens in a glass-bottomed boat.

Even before the boat's motor was cut, I could hear a number of birds. The first ones I saw were bananaquits followed closely by a gray kingbird singing from the top of a tree. I headed inland to spend a few minutes checking out the island's birds while my two companions combed the beach. Along one of the trails that criss-crossed the islands I heard a call which I believed to be that of the mangrove cuckoo although I never could locate the bird in the thick vegetation. But while searching for it, I looked up into the unblinking eyes of a yellow-crowned night heron not eight feet away. I guess you could say he was more patient than I as when I quietly backed away, he was still unmoved and staring. To defend myself, I will say that I knew my time to bird the island was limited.

It was on Rose Island where I encountered the sociable Swainson's warbler foraging low in the trees and shrubs in an opening in the jungle growth, occasionally hopping around on the ground. The dark russet head, white line over the eye and dusky streak through it, olive back, and light unstreaked underparts were all clearly visible. I lingered several minutes, reluctant to leave a scenario that might never again be enacted for me. When I came back up the trail about 15 minutes later, my warbler friend was still there, showing little concern for my passing.

The last morning of our stay in the Bahamas afforded the most productive birding, in both species and numbers, for the entire trip. While riding in a taxi on Paradise Island earlier in the week I had seen a small pond in the center of the island and determined to find an opportunity to bird it. Assuring my apprehensive husband that I would be back in time for our plane, I hiked the one and a half miles from our hotel and over the bridge to Paradise Island. The pond was everything I had hoped it to be. Common moorhens were abundant and they too were exhibiting the tameness I had found in so many of the Bahama birds. But winning the blue ribbon for fearlessness was the green-backed heron that I photographed repeatedly moving closer and closer, at about six feet away to have gotten any closer I would have been in the water.

Searching for a trail through the undergrowth to get to the other side, I finally got my first really good look at a male Bahama woodstar. My field guide had said these birds were supposed to be very tame and indifferent to the presence of humans. Apparently I had at last located one who had read the book. He posed closeup on an outer branch of a low shrub and turned from side to side to display the beauty of his iridescent violet gorget.

Unable to find a trail, I simply ducked down and scrambled through the dense undergrowth to reach my destination. Luckily there were no thorny vines such as smilax or blackberry which I would have encountered back home. My efforts were rewarded by the abundant bird life in this end of the pond away from the traffic that crossed the bridge at the other end.

I spent my last hour afield in the Bahamas, sitting on a flat rock in a birder's paradise on Paradise Island watching least and pied-billed grebes, a little blue heron, blue-winged teal, ruddy ducks, lesser scaup, a couple of great blue herons, a glossy ibis, Bahama ducks, (formerly known as Bahama pintails or white-cheeked pintails), American widgeons, and a tri-colored heron which is locally called a Poor Joe.

In addition to the pond itself, the area nearby yielded several species of warblers I had seen earlier in the week, as well as black-faced and melodious grasssquits, mourning doves which are locally called Florida doves, and my last new bird for the trip, a Key West quail dove. I saw the quail dove as I headed back to the bridge across to New Providence.

After our return home, a friend asked a member of our group who she thought had had the most fun on our trip. My sister-in-law replied, "I guess I would have to say Loice did. She put in longer hours and worked harder at it than any of the rest of us." It did indeed take constant effort to slip in a little birding in order not to interfere with our other plans. But going on a non-birding trip and adding 17 new birds to my life list, plus having several friendly encounters with some known skulkers, was worth the effort.

THE NEIGHBORLY INCAS

The bird books all say that inca doves nest near human habitation, sometimes on beams of open buildings or on other artificial supports. The pair that nested for four seasons atop a v-shaped bracket mounting a floodlight over a driveway in San Marcos, Texas, were sticklers for following the book. Otherwise, why would they have passed up the verdant acre of sloping woodland across the street to swelter in the heat of a sunny western exposure on the side of a house?

I first became aware of the Becker's avian tenants in November of 1982 when my brother-in-law, Buster, mentioned that "his" doves had just fledged their last brood of the season the previous month. The small, sociable, scaly-backed incas have a prolonged nesting season lasting from February to October, as do all dove species. This pair, again following the book, had begun their family duties in late February and had continued nesting repeatedly throughout the season. Buster told me that what he thought to be the same two doves, had built the nest the previous year and had used it for several broods that year.

When my sister, Tommye, told me in early April of 1983 that their inca doves were back again, we decided to keep a record of the nesting activities. As I live in Louisiana, she and her husband would observe the birds and keep me posted with phone calls and letters. We began with the April brood because, although they knew there had been activity at the nest in February as there had been the prior two years, they could not be sure any young had been produced. The April nesting resulted in two babies leaving the nest, appropriately enough, on Mother's Day.

During April, I went to San Marcos for a visit and while there took some photographs of the female dove on the nest. Aware that the birds never seemed to be disturbed by human presence, we didn't know the full extent of their tameness until this photographic session.

I was up on a ladder in the bed of a pickup truck parked in the driveway beneath the nest, with my tripod on top of the cab. All set for the perfect close-up and the bird wouldn't cooperate. Now I wasn't asking for any top-model posing, just that she would open her eyes and look alive. Buster would bang on the truck, wave his arms and jump up and down to awaken her for a picture. By the time I moved my equipment around to photograph at another angle, she would again have her eyes closed in sleep. Granted incubation to be a boring task, it would seem our curious actions would have shaken her out of the doldrums for the time being.

Even though the dove chose to ignore us, I think it probable that our peculiar activities had the full attention of the neighbors. Since the dove was unmoved by our presence at a distance of 6 to 8 feet, we decided to go up on the roof for an extremely close shot from above.

Here I was, lying on my tummy with my body parallel with the very edge of the roof. Buster was keeping a safe distance back, but tenaciously clinging to my sneakered feet, meanwhile cautioning me that the pavement could be hard after an 18-foot drop. Just as I leaned over the edge as far as I dared and positioned my camera lens only a few inches from the dove, she opened her eyes. Eyeball-to-eyeball was too much for her, she exploded from the nest and swooshed across the street to the serenity of the woods, leaving me with a close-up of two elliptical, glossy white eggs.

On May 10, only two days after the Mother's Day fledging, the dove was back on the nest early in the morning, cackling like a chicken according to my sister. Now I know the authorities who write the bird field guides make no mention of inca doves cackling, but our particular dove cackled. Permit her this one deviation from the book.

The dove was on the nest for a longer time on May 11, cackling from time to time, and finally a repeat of this ritual on May 12 produced the first egg of a usual two-egg clutch. The chicks from this nesting were uneventfully fledged June 8, exactly one month after those of the previous brood.

Strangely, at no time during the months of observation were the birds seen adding to the nest. However, the location of the nest is such that one can see it only by going around on the west side of the house. Since the bulky stick platform precariously mounted on its metal support is far larger than the few flimsy sticks which comprise the usual dove nest, it likely was the product of perennial construction. The male could have been bringing her a stick occasionally to shore up a weak spot or a bit of fine plant down to soften the lining. Doves often forego the luxury of any lining at all. While both sexes share in nest building, she doesn't trust him as an artisan. He brings the materials, she arranges them.

The dove was back on the nest cackling again on June 10. This time the sitting on the nest for long periods of time and the intermittent cackling lasted four days before an egg was laid. The next day a second egg was added and after 13 days of incubation, both eggs hatched.

Following the fledging of the baby doves on July 12, days passed with no sign of the parent birds. If they were taking a well-deserved vacation by some clear sparkling lake, or resting from their domestic toils in the seclusion of a wooded glade, our anxiety could have been relieved with the trite message "Having a good time. Wish you were here."

INCA DOVES

We thought of the cooler area across the street from the house, an acre of what was, to our thinking, a virtual dove paradise dotted with elms and cedars, and abounding with grass and weed seeds, Much as we'd miss the birds, we almost wished they wouldn't renew their lease on the bracket because of the increasing heat of the July days.

But eight days after the last fledging, vacation over, the parent doves were again at the old nest. By now the temperatures were ranging well over the hundred mark daily and the heat radiating from the metal in the vicinity of the nest must have pushed the temperature even higher. The protection of the parent dove's body during incubation would be needed to shield the eggs from the heat rather than to keep them warm. Again we worried. Would the inca doves, even though their range is from the hot, arid southwestern United States to northwestern Costa Rica, be able to tolerate excessive heat on the nest?. Not to worry. Again two baby doves were hatched. After two weeks in the nest gorging themselves on pigeon's milk, which is a partly digested food from the crops of the parent birds, the babies left the nest.

Often a rain in August in Southwest Texas can bring cooler weather for the remainder of the summer. It was perhaps with this in mind that the female dove made a decision to return to the nest, this time in only three days. Or maybe she was going for some kind of record. After all, this would be her fifth, or maybe sixth if there was a February nesting, with two babies fledged each time. Although four or five broods are not uncommon for doves, generally only about 50 percent of nestings are successful due to the toll of weather, predators, and sometimes the bird's own carelessness in construction of a nest too shoddy to keep the eggs from rolling out.

Even though our doves had extreme heat with which to contend, their nest did have some protection from the elements being near to the wall of the house and slightly under the eaves. In addition, having human neighbors gave safety from predation. Perhaps in enumerating what our doves had going for them, I've answered our questions about the wisdom of their choice of a nesting site.

After a couple of days back at the nest, the female sitting on it and cackling from time to time, left without producing an egg. For whatever reason, the nesting season at this site seemed to be over for our doves. Maybe he persuaded her to let someone else be featured in the Guinness Book of World Records. Or perhaps he enticed her with glowing descriptions of the new nest they could build across the street in the cool of a sheltering elm.

After an absence of six months which we feared would be permanent, the doves were back at the nest atop the light bracket in mid-February talking about remodeling. Although no structural changes were apparent, she must have been content to make-do as within a week she was doing her sitting and cackling routine. Two days later she laid her first of her two eggs, but this time only one nestling fledged. The other egg was found on the pavement beneath the nest during the incubation period.

After the nest was vacated in February the birds never returned. Throughout the1984 nesting season, the Beckers hopefully watched the nest for signs of activity. Among the doves coo-cooing in the trees across the street and feeding in the gravel beside the road, they repeatedly searched for their parent doves, but never could be certain of identification.

Their last hope for return of their doves was dashed when February of 1985 passed with no sign of activity at the old nest. It still balances on the light bracket, appearing as sturdy as when first built over four years ago, showing little wear from the ravages of time and weather and the rearing of over two dozen nestlings. On a scale of 1 to 10, I would rate it a 10. Perhaps our doves are now nesting in heaven to the delight of nature lovers up there.

GEMS AND GYMNASTS OF THE BIRD WORLD

Ornately decorated in beautiful iridescent colors, hummingbirds have been fondly called "glittering fragments of the rainbow" by John James Audubon. Many tropical species are named for precious gems because of the jewel-like throat feathers, called gorgets, of the males. Varying with the species, the gorget may be flaming red, red-violet, blue, purple, or green. Although 18 species come regularly to the United States in the spring, the ruby-throated hummingbird is the only one common in the east and the sole one to breed east of the Great Plains.

Hummingbirds are aerial gymnasts capable of flying backward, upward, darting, or hovering stationary in the manner of a helicopter. Their wings beat as fast as 60 times a second, creating the sound which gives them their name. The smallest of all birds, with a three inch length and a weight less than that of a penny, a hummingbird has stronger wings for its size than any other bird. It is able to fly over 500 miles non-stop when migrating across the Gulf of Mexico. To survive the long migratory journey, the tiny hummer builds an energy reserve by gaining weight just prior to departure.

Hummingbirds return to their nesting grounds early in the spring and immediately the males begin their courtships with great flair. Unable to sing – they use their voices for squeaking when angry or frightened – they attempt dazzling aerial maneuvers to woo their mates. The ruby-throated male in display swings in a wide arc like a pendulum, each swing accompanied by a hum. Having won his lady fair, the male shirks all marital duties, leaving the building of the nest, incubating of the eggs, and feeding of the young to the female. Meantime the polygamous male mates with other females.

The nest of the ruby-throated hummingbird is usually saddled on the fork of a downward sloping twig, commonly 10 to 20 feet up in a tree or shrub. It is built of small fragments of plant material with a thick lining of down, and bound together tightly with spider webs, then covered on the outside with flakes of lichens. Camouflaged to look like a knot on a branch, the whole nest is not much larger than half of an English walnut. The two smooth white pea-sized eggs hatch in 16 days. The young, which are fed by the insertion of the parent's food-filled bill into their mouths, are ready to leave the nest in approximately 19 days.

In the earliest ornithological studies it was believed that the dainty hummingbird found the nectar from flowers ample nourishment for its active life, but more recent studies prove it to be an insect eater of ravenous appetite. The relative proportion of nectar and insects consumed is difficult to appraise even though extensive tests have been conducted. In one such test, stomach examinations of 230 specimens showed almost nothing but insects, although some hummers were collected while feeding from flower to flower. The nectar was either immediately digested or its presence was not detected for unknown reasons. The most common insects found in the stomachs were small flies, ants, beetles and bees. Presumably, hummingbirds feeding among flowers are partaking of both meat and drink. In addition, the hummers drink the sap oozing from trees and also sip the juice of some fruits.

HUMMINGBIRD IN HAND

The old saying "A bird in the hand is worth two in the bush" may have been penned in reference to hummingbirds. There's no better way to get a good view of these active and energetic little avian jewels.

Because hummingbirds have a high rate of metabolism, it is necessary for them to feed as often as every 15 minutes. Their daytime body temperature is around 113 degrees, but with cessation of activity at night, it drops to 65 degrees. With this low temperature, the birds enter a state of semi-hibernation which conserves energy when they are unable to feed constantly.

Appreciated chiefly for their dazzling beauty, hummingbirds are beneficial in the pollination of flowers as they flit from one to another seeking nectar and insects. The slender beak, which is usually half the length of the body in an adult hummer, is especially adapted for probing the tubular flowers the birds favor. The long tongue has the outer edges curved forming two tubes with minute brushes at the tip which are useful in sucking up nectar as well as sweeping up insects.

In addition to a garden of their favorite flowers, the birds appreciate having their diet supplemented with sweetened water from a hummingbird feeder. The nectar can be purchased or prepared by boiling a mixture of one part sugar and four parts water. No red food coloring is needed as feeders are always designed with red on them. Actually, food coloring has been found to be toxic to the birds. Don't take down your feeders until you stop seeing the hummers. They usually migrate south for their winter vacation near the end of October and return to their breeding grounds early in March.

Although not all people are as successful as a lady in Monroe, Louisiana, who feeds hummingbirds from a vial held between her lips, enticing the tiny iridescent gems to frequent yards holds universal interest. From March to October, rare is the garden that offers blooming flowers or man-made feeders that isn't visited by hummingbirds.

EL PAISANO MOVES EASTWARD

Faster than a four-minute miler, the roadrunner races up and down roads from California south to Central Mexico and east to western Louisiana and Arkansas. His antics in real life are no less astounding and comical than those the roadrunner performs in popular movie cartoons.

The roadrunner, a ground-dwelling cuckoo, got its name in early days running down roads ahead of horses or horse-drawn vehicles. It is also called lizard bird, chaparral cock, running cuckoo, cock of the desert and snake bird. Perhaps the most befitting name of a bird so beloved by the natives of the southwest where its populations are the densest is el paisano, meaning "fellow countryman" in Spanish.

The very appearance of the roadrunner makes him a natural for cartoon characterization. His mixed-up plumage of metallic green, purple, black, with predominate brown and white, is set off by blue and orange on bare areas of his face. Even in baby roadrunners the expressive yellow-orange eyes are encircled by long lashes. A jaunty, bristle-tipped crest and a two-inch rapier beak are other distinctive features.

ROADRUNNER

Because the roadrunner has two toes pointing forward and two pointing backward it is impossible to tell by his tracks whether he is coming or going. The Indians scratched facsimiles of his odd tracks near the graves of the departed to confuse the evil spirits. Mexicans and Indians of the Southwest encourage El Paisano to nest near their homes to ensure good luck. Often mothers tie its feathers to the cradles of their babies to ward off evil.

Many strange stories surround the roadrunner, a creature of such bizarre behavior that almost anything seems plausible. One tall tale describes how the birds build fences made of sharp cactus spines around sleeping rattlesnakes. In trying to free himself, the imprisoned reptile will die as he becomes impaled on the spiny barbs. The ways roadrunners are known to outwit rattlesnakes are equally astonishing. Cunning El Paisano is among the few animals on the desert that will challenge a deadly rattler.

As the teasing bird dances around, always keeping just out of reach and sometimes kicking sand in the reptile's eyes with a little below the belt strategy, the snake is encouraged to keep striking until exhausted. The bird then swiftly closes in, pecks out the victim's eyes and finishes him off with his rapier bill.

Snakes and other large prey of the roadrunner are slammed against such hard surfaces as rocks, sticks, firm ground, and even tin cans to render them palatable. Large animals are always swallowed headfirst and often a roadrunner can be seen running around with the tail of a lizard or snake dangling from the bird's mouth until a rapid digestive process permits the remainder to be swallowed.

While population densities are highest in the more open areas of its range, the roadrunner has extended its territory eastward, having first been sighted in Louisiana and Arkansas in the late 1930s. An old belief persists that the birds did not appear in Louisiana until a bridge was built across the Sabine River permitting them to walk across from Texas. Actually the roadrunner can fly short distances in a sort of extended bounce, yet he prefers to run at tremendous speeds of up to 15 to 20 miles per hour. The short rounded wings which take the weight off the feet and the foot-long tail are designed for balance and maneuverability as the bird skims across the ground with his feet barely touching the surface. With powerful leg muscles allowing long strides, he runs entirely on tiptoe, knees bent back and held high. The bird's long narrow tail can be thrown in the air to brake suddenly and a wing can be spread for a quick turn.

Pair bonds among roadrunners are apparently "until death do us part." In the spring at sunrise, the male bird goes to the rim of a mesa or perches on a dead tree or cactus to sing his hoarse, throaty courtship coo, coo, ooh, ooh, raising his head slightly with each note. Roadrunners also make clacking noises with their bills and utter purring perrp, perrp, perrp sounds.

The roadrunner nest is built in a cactus, low shrub or tree, or rarely on the ground. The foundation of the compact cup that is about a foot in diameter is of twigs with a lining of such things as leaves, roots, feathers, snake skins, mesquite pods, and dry pieces of horse and cattle manure. The white eggs may number 3 to 12 with the larger number being from more than one female using the same nest. Because incubation begins as soon as the first egg is laid, a nest may contain eggs and young of various ages.

The bird that favors lizards, spiders, mice, and small snakes, with practically no plant material in its diet, does occasionally relish small birds and eggs. A Texas birder once observed a roadrunner halfway up a large mesquite tree heckling a pair of scissor-tailed flycatchers that were defending their nest, noisily shrieking and scolding as they dive-bombed the intruder. The bird that dances fearlessly just out of reach of a deadly rattlesnake then moves in for the kill, slunk away in meek defeat before the persistent onslaught of the dauntless flycatchers. No eggs or baby birds for lunch that day.

As a roadrunner races down a country road, it takes only a little imagination to hear his "beep, beep" as he maneuvers to right or left with outstretched wing or screeches to a halt with tail flung high. And if you see a long, streamlined bird skimming on tiptoe across a Mississippi River bridge, you'll know it is El

Paisano extending his range by the easiest route to make friends with his fellow-countrymen east of the Big Muddy.

EXTENDING THEIR RANGE

Many birds and other animals are extending their range by appearing in areas where they had never been sighted before. The first official record of a flock of tree sparrows was established in Louisiana when a flock was found wintering at the country home of John and Martha Harson near Haynesville, Louisiana. Prior to this a single bird had been sighted occasionally with four having been seen a few times. The times they were recorded as being seen were in 1904, 1940, 1954 and 1958.

These tiny birds nest in northern Canada and usually winter no farther south than the central United States. They remained at the Harsons for a long time and were expected to stay there if food supply was ample until nesting time in late March or early April. Two of the birds were mounted by my son, Don Kendrick, for the Wildlife Museum at Louisiana Tech in Ruston where he was a student.

Inca doves, formerly a bird of Central America, Mexico and the southwestern United States, first appeared in the southeastern United States in 1968. Semi-tropical white-winged doves also appeared in Louisiana about the same time. Before this time their range had been the same as that of the inca doves.

Eurasian collared doves escaped from a pet shop in the Bahamas during a burglary in the mid-1970s in the shop. The owner of the pet shop then released the remaining birds which was about 50. Native to Europe and Asia, the doves were first documented as breeding in Florida in 1982. Since about 2000, they have spread rapidly across the continent.

House sparrows were released in Brooklyn, New York, in 1851. They were brought to the United States as some expected they would destroy a caterpillar that was defoliating elm trees on the east coast. These alien birds had spread rapidly to the Rocky Mountains by 1900.

The first armadillo was reported as seen in Louisiana in 1936. As this animal can't swim to get across the Sabine River from Texas, it had to figure out another way to cross the river. They can walk across on the river bottom or another way is to gulp large amounts of air to inflate their lungs and intestines in order to be able to float across a body of water.

ARMADILLO

House finches are native to Mexico and the southern United States. Caged birds released in 1940 in New York spread quickly across the continent. Not nearly as welcome here by birders is the European starling. It was brought to New York Central Park in the early 1890s. This release was by a group who wanted North America to have all the birds ever mentioned by William Shakespeare. This loathed bird pushes out native cavity nesters such as bluebirds, woodpeckers, owls, purple martins, tree swallows and flycatchers.

THREATENED OR EXTINCT SPECIES

Over 190 species of birds have become extinct since 1500. It's possible that our next two birds to become extinct may be the California condor and the snowy owl. Currently, this condor, whooping crane and the red-cockaded woodpecker are on the endangered species list. The California condor has the longest wingspread of any bird in the United States, measuring 120 inches.

The red-cockaded woodpecker has been listed as endangered since the 1970s. There are currently less than 15,000 in the United States. Predators and lack of sufficient places to nest and roost are major problems for them. Hawks, rat snakes and flying squirrels prey upon eggs and nestlings. These birds use live pines for nesting and roosting. Such trees need to be more than 80 years old and are often infected with heart rot fungus.

The ivory-billed woodpecker that was declared extinct in 2021 is the latest for the United States. President Teddy Roosevelt was the first person to call this woodpecker "The Lord God bird." He was on a hunting trip to Northern Louisiana in 1907 when he spotted three of these birds on land that would become known as the Singer tract. The size of the woodpecker caused him to exclaim, "Lord God, what a bird!"

On a different subject, when Roosevelt was on a 1902 hunting trip in Mississippi, he refused to shoot a bear that had been conked on the head and tied to a tree. This resulted in the "Teddy Bear" being created in his honor. Teddy Roosevelt was known for his concern for all things of nature throughout his life. We could use his help now to address conservation and environmental problems.

Now back to the ivory-billed which is the largest woodpecker in North America and the third largest in the world. Destruction of old-growth forests in the 1800s caused severe population declines for this woodpecker and by the

20th century very few remained. The 21th century marked the time of its being declared extinct in the United States.

This woodpecker was reported as last seen in Louisiana in the 1940s. I was present at an Arkansas Audubon Society meeting in early May of 2005 when the announcement was made that an ivory-billed woodpecker had just been seen and photographed in April in a bottom-land swamp forest of Arkansas. Over 50 experts and field biologists working together and backed by the Cornell Laboratory of Ornithology filmed a video of the bird.

The bald eagle was once on the endangered species list. Its populations were declining due to habitat destruction, illegal shootings and the use of pesticides, chiefly DDT. After DDT was banned in 1972 and laws began being passed to protect habitat and criminalize shootings, bald eagles are now thriving. A true success story!

BALD EAGLE

Some populations of birds and other animals grow while others dwindle. The wild turkey, the bird that Benjamin Franklin wanted to be our national symbol, has ebbed and flowed in its populations. Prior to 1880 as many as one million wild turkeys inhabited Louisiana. However, by the turn of the century, the state's population was drastically reduced. Timber production and unrestricted hunting played a role in the decline. By 1946, there were fewer than 1,500 wild turkeys in Louisiana. With the enacting of a restoration program in 1962, the populations have grown slowly to an estimated 80,000.

The bobwhite has all but disappeared from Louisiana despite efforts by the Wildlife and Fisheries Commission to reestablish the small bird. Several things may have contributed to the decline such as an increase in the numbers of its predators, the infiltration of fire ants and the replacement of natural forest by pine plantations.

Also, roadrunners, killdeer and other birds that were once common here, are now less often seen. Gray squirrels have mostly replaced the larger reddish fox squirrel. (I would like to see both species disappear as they bite into my pecans while they are still green. Thus my harvest is depleted). Many years ago black bears could not have been expected to be seen in Louisiana. Wildlife management practices have brought the bear population up. For instance, a black bear was spotted several years ago by a citizen of Haynesville, Louisiana, who's yard backed up to a wooded area.

Back in the 1930s and '40s, deer were rarely seen in Louisiana because much of the area was sparsely forested as the land was used for growing cotton and food crops. Now with the planting of many trees on land formerly used to grow crops our woods are heavily populated with deer.

For many years horned toads thrived in Texas. Having grown up in the country in West Texas, I can vouch for that. I got more than my share of stings by the red ants on which the toads feed. There would be several ant beds in our yard with toads sitting in the middle of the beds eating ants. These toads are also called horny toads, horned frogs, and horned lizards. Actually, they are lizards and not toads nor frogs.

HORNED TOAD

There is a legend, which to me is not believable, that in 1897 a capsule containing a horned toad was placed in the cornerstone of a courthouse being built in Eastland, Texas. In 1928 a bigger courthouse was needed so the old one was torn down. To everyone's astonishment, the dusty critter buried 31 years ago was still alive. They called him "Ol Rip" after Rip Van Winkle. It makes a good story whether or not you believe it.

It is thought that populations of the horned toad began to decline because of urbanization, pesticides and the arrival of fire ants. By the 21th century, the populations of the beloved horned toad had dwindled so much that extensive efforts were begun to save it. In 2018 the first of the toads captive-bred at the Fort Worth Zoo were released as hatchlings into the wild. These hibernated through the winter and were alive the next spring. In all, 132 were released that year.

The Texas horned toad was designated as the state reptile in 1993. The Horned Lizard Society was formed sometime in the 1900s to work on conservation of the horned lizard. Those members plus teams from many Texas zoos, Texas Parks and Wildlife and Texas Christian University have pioneered care and breeding techniques for wild-caught horned lizards. Now the future is becoming to look much brighter for the Texas state reptile.

A TIME TO GO

Salmon battle incredible odds to swim upstream in the spring and birds fly long distances, overcoming difficult obstacles, following the urge to change location with the stirrings of the migratory seasons. In early biblical times, the prophet Jeremiah noted that "the stork in heaven knoweth her appointed times, and the turtle and the crane and the swallow observe the time of their coming."

Migration, defined as any movement between two locations, is undertaken by many animals, especially those in which locomotion is exceptionally well developed and the animals are susceptible to marked changes in their environment. Birds are outstanding migrants because they can travel great distances with comparative ease and are completely dependent on their environment for food, shelter and breeding sites.

The phenomenon of seasonal migration was first observed in birds long before there was any understanding of it. Aristotle advanced the theory that most birds went into hiding at certain seasons or underwent transmutation, while many Europeans believed some birds wintered on the moon. As recently as two centuries ago, respected scientists proclaimed that swallows spent the winter hibernating in marsh mud.

Synchronized with the annual seasonal changes, migration does not take place until birds are properly prepared and stimulated. Day-length affects the pituitary gland resulting in a condition termed "migratory restlessness." Preparation for migration involves storing of energy to meet the requirements of prolonged flight. Food eaten in excess of a bird's daily needs is stored as energy in the form of subcutaneous fat. For example, a ruby-throated hummingbird increases its body fat content to over five times as much as normal. This fat is about half of its entire weight and is needed for an astounding 500-mile nonstop flight across the Gulf of Mexico.

Fall migration is more prolonged than that of spring with less regularity in arrival and departure. Cool weather in late summer may trigger early migration and warm weather may cause birds to linger beyond their usual departure time. In spring the urgency to reach their breeding grounds results in more rapid and punctual migration.

Many birds such as loons, geese, ducks, gulls, terns and shore birds travel by either day or night. Herons, hawks, eagles, crows, swifts, swallows, and hummingbirds migrate solely by day. One of the explanations advanced for nocturnal flight is that it affords birds that normally live in dense vegetation the protection of darkness against their diurnal predators. Another is that it enables birds to use daylight hours for feeding to replenish their energy reserves.

BULLOCK'S ORIOLE

Most passerine birds travel at ground-speeds averaging 18 to 25 miles per hour while stronger flyers such as ducks, geese, hawks, and shore birds attain much higher speeds. In one test, an airplane pilot traveling at an air-speed of 90 miles per hour was overtaken by two flocks of sandpipers flying at an estimated speed of 110 miles per hour.

Analysis of migratory flight by radar shows that birds fly higher by night than by day and higher over land than sea. The altitude may be determined by cloud cover as birds tend to fly higher when skies are overcast in an attempt to get above the clouds. Although the most frequent height is 1,500 to 2,500 feet, and most birds rarely exceed 8,000 to 10,000 feet, a yellow-billed chough was found on Mt. Everest at an elevation of 27,000 feet.

Distances covered by migrating birds range from as little as several hundred feet traveled by high-mountain species moving up and down slopes to thousands of miles for the Arctic tern, which makes the longest migratory flight of any bird. This species nests as far north as 83 degrees North Latitude and has been found as far south as 74 degrees South Latitude. Its migration takes it from one polar region to another. Distances of migration do not appear to be correlated to size or flight abilities. A number of small species migrate to Mexico and Central America, a longer journey than is undertaken by many larger species which would seem to have greater capabilities for lengthy flights.

Migration is dangerous for all birds and has become more so because of many hazards created by man. Birds are attracted by light and often are killed by colliding with lighthouses, tall buildings, television towers, and sometimes even street lights. Severe storms also take a toll of the migratory populations. In addition, birds forced to land by a cold front may become victims of predators because of lack of adequate cover.

Although migration is a subject long steeped in magic and myth, modern scientists are now uncovering startling facts about how creatures find their way around. In addition to the probability that many species of migratory birds inherit ability to find their way, scientists also grant that some ability is acquired by experience and that other aids to direction-finding include celestial bodies and the wind. In the last decade many scientists have accepted the idea that birds, as well as other creatures, can detect and orient themselves to magnetic fields such as that of the earth. In the late 1950s, researchers in Germany discovered that European robins in an indoor cage where they were unable to see the sun or stars knew which way to migrate. In the wild, these birds travel from Germany to Spain in the fall. As caged birds, they developed a migratory restlessness always attempting to fly toward the southwest as they would have done in normal migration.

Magnetite, the material from which the first compasses were made, has been discovered in an odd form of highly migratory bacteria living in marsh mud, in the abdomens of bees, and in the heads of pigeons. No definite conclusions can be drawn, but the possibility of a link between the magnetite and these animals' unerring migratory ability seems likely.

According to one ornithologist, a bird in migration must not only know where it is, it must know the direction of its goal, it must be able to navigate its course in that direction, and stop when it reaches its destination. Uncovering scientific explanations as to how birds possess such complex migratory abilities can make the long flights of a tiny hummingbird that ordinarily must feed every 15 minutes no less astounding. Nor detract from the magnitude of the 10,000-mile marathon of the globe-trotting Arctic tern.

As surely as the subtle changing of the seasons signals the time to go, both bird and bird enthusiast are stimulated by the awesome and enthralling stirrings of the migratory period.

PLAY HOST TO THE BUTTERFLIES

I will begin this chapter with a quote by Nathaniel Hawthorne, "Happiness is a butterfly, which when pursued, is always just beyond your reach, but which, if you sit down quietly, may alight upon you."

Winter and early spring are good times to establish host plants for the butterflies. Host plants are those on which butterflies deposit their eggs and on which the caterpillars feed. Butterflies go through three stages of metamorphosis before emerging as butterflies. Those stages are egg, caterpillar and chrysalis. Caterpillars of some species are very selective, only using plants of a particular genus, while others will accept species from more than one plant family. Although most yards will have existing plants on which some kinds of caterpillars feed, the inclusion of others of different species will insure a wider variety of butterflies to enjoy.

GULF FRITILLARY IN J-SHAPE

Years ago, when I was giving a program on butterflies to a group in Shreveport, Louisiana, one woman told me she didn't want "those old worms", she just wanted the butterflies. Like the words of the old song "Love and Marriage", you can't have one without the other. There are many host plants easily established by either seeds or transplants for those "old worms." I will list some of them here, each followed by the butterflies hosted: milkweed, monarch; any citrus such as prickly-ash or rue, giant swallowtail; tulip poplar, tiger swallowtail and spicebush swallowtail; hackberry, tawny and hackberry emperor, mourning cloak, question mark, and snout; willow, viceroy, red-spotted purple, mourning cloak, and tiger swallowtail; sassafras, spicebush and palamedes swallowtails; spicebush, spicebush swallowtail; hollyhock and hibiscus, painted lady, checkered skipper and gray hairstreak; asters, pearl crescent and American painted lady; passion flower, zebra longwing, Gulf and variegated fritillaries; pansies and violas, variegated and other fritillaries; fennel, dill, Queen Annes lace and other members of the parsley family, black swallowtail; legumes such as partridge pea, clover and vetch, all larvae of sulphur species; hops, Eastern comma, question mark; pawpaw, zebra swallowtail. And that mistletoe that you thought was only good for standing under at Christmas time all puckered up for a kiss, hosts the great purple hairstreak. Of course this list is only partial, but butterfly books will give you even more information. My children have been known to say that they doubt I'm growing hops for caterpillars, but I've yet to learn how to use it to brew beer.

BLACK SWALLOWTAIL CATERPILLARS ON FENNEL

60

One year at the annual Haynesville Celebration of Butterflies festival, we had so many Gulf fritillary and other species of caterpillars on plants in the butterfly conservatory that one woman exclaimed, "Somebody better get in here and spray. These plants are just covered with worms!" And we had been so pleased to have great numbers of various caterpillars to show to the festival attendees. (Actually, not all butterfly larvae feed on plants. The harvester butterfly larvae are carnivorous, feeding on wooly aphids found on aspens and various other trees.) To set the record straight, caterpillars are not worms, even though this woman and the one in Shreveport both called them that. One year at the festival we had a zebra swallowtail that was netted by a friend out in the country. Most attendees said they had never before seen this butterfly species.

ZEBRA SWALLOWTAIL

As you will note, many trees and shrubs are useful as host plants for butterflies, but they should be placed so that they do not shade out the sun-loving flowers, the nectar of which feeds the butterflies. The inclusion of trees and shrubs in your yard also furnishes shelter at night and during inclement weather for the butterflies. Possibly your neighbors will also have trees and other plants that will give shelter and feed your caterpillars.

As butterflies seek nectar, they are also pollinating as they move from blossom to blossom. Among the flowering plants that attract butterflies are zinnias, cosmos, purple coneflower, gaillardia, salvias, bachelor buttons, asters, sunflower, goldenrod, verbena, lantana, impatiens, petunias, buddleia, coreopsis, larkspur, monarda, and the list goes on and on. Also, many of the host plants do double-duty as nectar plants. Do not spray pesticides because that will destroy your larvae and butterflies. If a spray is necessary to get rid of some pests in your butterfly garden, you can use a strong spray of water or simply pick them off and destroy them. Happy butterfly gardening!

THE MAJESTIC MONARCHS

All that is tawny-gold and brown and flutters on the autumn breeze is not falling leaves. Vast numbers of monarch butterflies on the wing are fall's faithful harbingers as they begin their migration south for their winter vacation.

Considered majestic in the insect world because of its large size and spectacular beauty, the monarch is the only butterfly to engage in true seasonal migration, sometimes covering phenomenal distances. In a tagging survey conducted by the Milwaukee Public Museum, one monarch was traced from Wisconsin to Southern Georgia, a distance of nearly 1,000 miles. Another of this species tagged by the Toronto Museum was tracked some 1,870 miles from Canada to Mexico.

Monarchs are natives of North America, but have been found in Great Britain and elsewhere in Europe. They have never gained a foothold there because of the absence of milkweeds, the host plants for the caterpillars. It has not been determined if the butterflies got across the ocean by their own wing power or were stowaways on a ship. However, monarchs have been seen flying far out to sea, so they could have flown to Europe.

With the first nightly drops in temperature in the north, usually occurring in late August or early September, the monarchs begin assembling in their breeding grounds as far north as Canada for their annual trek to their wintering sites in California or Mexico. Gathering in large swarms in fields and open woodlands, they feed on nectar of fall flowers such as sunflowers, asters, coneflowers and goldenrods, storing energy for their long trip south. Having supped sufficiently, they gather on a chosen tree in such hordes that the tree appears to have changed foliage.

In some areas the monarchs assemble year after year in the same precise spot. This occurs to such a marked extent in California that it has been called "an entomological Capistrano." As butterflies prefer to travel over land rather than water, there is usually a greater concentration of migratory flights in shore areas, especially near the Great Lakes and along the Atlantic and Pacific regions.

After the start of a flight south, the monarchs are joined by others as they are on the wing. They do not fly in a definite formation as do ducks and geese, but sail along in a scattered manner at a height of from 50 to several hundred feet. The monarch does not flutter its wings in flight, but after a few strong full wing strokes, it glides gracefully for a long distance. Capable of regulating its speed, it may travel very rapidly when on protracted flights.

In their winter quarters, the monarchs cluster motionless high up in trees in a semi-torpid state, fluttering only on warm sunny days. Their immobility in cold weather is similar to the hibernation of non-migrating species of butterflies that winter in the northern United States and Canada.

Unlike the massed fall migration, in early spring the monarchs fly northward individually as if each is attuned to its own singular timing device urging it back to the breeding grounds. The females may stop on the way to lay their numerous pale green eggs on any of the milkweed plants found along the route. These eggs will result in butterflies that will continue the northward journey.

The metamorphosis of the monarch through its four stages is typical of all butterflies. The eggs deposited on milkweeds will hatch into small black and white larvae in about three weeks, The caterpillars eat their way out of the eggs, often consuming the shell as their first meal. They shed their skins several times in the course of the two or three weeks it takes to become fully grown. When mature the caterpillars are about two inches long, with a yellow head crossed by two triangular stripes of black. The body is marked with narrow transverse stripes of yellow, orange, white and black, and adorned with four long shaking black horns called filaments.

At the mature stage the caterpillar stops eating, finds something from which it can hang and spins a layer of thin silk over the supporting surface. It hangs upside down from the silk pad, holding on with its back legs. Then the caterpillar's skin loosens, splits and is rolled upward revealing the pupa which has developed inside.

MONARCHS AND A CHRYSALIS

In its early form the pupa (chrysalis) is a smooth light green dotted with brilliant gold. Later it becomes brown and within a short time the bright orange wings of the butterfly can be seen through the transparent covering of the chrysalis.

Within two weeks from the beginning of the pupal stage, the monarch emerges from the chrysalis shell. It pushes its way to freedom and hangs upside down in order to expand the wings. It awaits the drying of its wings before it is able to fly. The phenomenon known as "red rain" may occur when large numbers of butterflies emerge in the same area. Soon after emerging, the butterflies secrete a drop or two of red liquid called meconium, which is nitrogen body waste formed in the chrysalis stage. When this is spattered over leaves and other surfaces it has the appearance of red raindrops.

When I wrote about monarchs for the Arkansas Audubon Society newsletter in 1981, I stated that it has been noted that while some 40 species of butterflies seem destined to be listed as endangered, the monarch is as prevalent as ever. That is no longer true as populations have declined over 90 percent in the past two decades. The destruction of milkweeds by herbicides, and climate impacts like rising temperatures, wildfires and drought are causing major problems for the monarchs.

We must do everything possible to combat climate change and to restore milkweeds to host the caterpillars. One can buy milkweed seeds or plants at nurseries. There are many native milkweed species and the tropical milkweed, also called Mexican milkweed, is hardy as far north as northern Louisiana. Monarch Watch, a research program based at the University of Kansas, has seeds and plants available. Go online to shop.milkweedmarket.org. They are free to schools, charities, etc and cost very little for others. Also, you can have your yard declared a Monarch Waystation if you have milkweeds and nectar plants for the monarchs. I have such a sign in my backyard butterfly garden.

THOMAS LEARNS ABOUT ECOLOGY

Thomas loved living in the country where he could enjoy all the birds and animals that lived in the woods and open land on his dad's acreage. His dad majored in wildlife biology in college and was able to teach him much about ecology.

The birds and other animals gathered in a circle to talk awhile before beginning their duties for the day. For a few minutes they all seemed deep in thought, then Blue Jay, who never could be quiet for long, spoke up, "I like living here because there are so many trees suitable for my nest and the oaks have such a good supply of acorns, which are my favorite food." Then Bluebird spoke in his quiet voice, "You'd never catch me building a nest on a tree limb in the open. I'm a cavity-nester which means I nest in some kind of safe place. Because my beak is not adapted for drilling, Woodpecker lets me use his holes once he is through with them. Also, I nest in natural tree cavities and in a man-made box like the one I'm sitting on now." Red-headed Woodpecker and Purple Martin both spoke up to say that nesting in cavities made them feel safer from predators.

One day Thomas went with his dad to feed the catfish in a pond. Great Egret was there feeding on aquatic animals like snails, frogs, fish, and aquatic insects. Egret said, "It amuses me that Thomas calls me Common Great American Egret. I like the sound of that name. Actually, my name has been changed several times by the Ornithologists' Union. I have been officially called American Egret, Great Egret and now Common Egret."

COMMON EGRET

"You think you have a lot of names! What about me?" a voice asked from some vegetation growing by the pond. Egret looked hard to spot American Bittern who had a habit of standing with his beak pointed skyward so that he was camouflaged by the cattails. Bittern continued, "Because of my peculiar call that has been described as sounding like an old hand-operated water pump, I have been called the water pump bird, the pumper, and thunder pumper. Some people call me dunk-a-doo because they think it sounds like what I'm saying when I call."

From a nearby fence post, Bobwhite spoke up, "It isn't any doubt what I'm saying when I call. I'll bet Thomas already knows me by my voice." Then Three-toed Box Turtle came slowly crawling across the dam. He said, "Although Thomas wouldn't know me by my voice as I'm very quiet, I'll bet he has known me longer than any other animal. By the time he was able to talk, he would look at me and call my name", Turtle boasted proudly.

Alligator Snapping Turtle was resting quietly on the bottom of the pond with his mouth open. He moved the pink worm-like structure on his tongue back and forth to attract prey. The pink flap looked just like a fishing lure. Snapping Turtle said, "Thomas hasn't known me as long as he has Box Turtle, but he talks about me a lot. He is afraid to swim here in the pond as he is scared I might bite him. I'm very impressive because of my size. We are the largest fresh-water turtles in the world with some of us exceeding two feet in length. The record weight for one of us is 219 pounds. That's more than Thomas' daddy weighs!"

Sometimes Thomas would climb up into one of his dad's deer stands and watch for animals in the area. One day Deer saw him up there but just kept feeding around close by. "I believe Thomas has known me as long as he has Box Turtle", said Deer. "I would like for him to learn more about what I like to eat. He could make a little game of learning to identify the plants I favor for food. By learning about botany perhaps he would get his dad to establish more of my preferred food plants here."

There was a small creek running through the land where Thomas liked to go view the animals there. One day, Raccoon who was still wet from having waded into the creek to catch a frog, now spoke up, "This creek is a great place to catch my prey and I like to wash my food there before I eat it." Deer agreed with Raccoon, saying, "Yes the creek is nice. I like to go there for a cool drink. And I enjoy going into the nearby woods to find young shoots, buds and such to eat." Deer's mouth was so crammed with food that he could barely be understood as he spoke.

Once when Thomas was down by the creek, he heard a loud "slap" that was Beaver taken by surprise as he was on the bank gnawing down a willow tree to add to his food supply and dam. He had quickly jumped in the creek, slapping the water with his tail to warn the other beavers that someone was around. Discovering that the intruder was their friend, Thomas, they went back to work on their lodge because, as you know, they are always "busy as a beaver".

Once when Thomas had gone down to the family's chicken houses, he spotted Possum there getting some dead chickens for supper. Possum said, "I may not be much to look at, but there are several things about me that might interest Thomas. Many people think that when I 'play possum' or appear to be dead that I'm just pretending. Actually, when I am frightened I go into a coma-like state. This is lucky for me as predators leave me alone as they are only interested in live prey. Another unusual thing about me is that I'm the only native North American marsupial. That means I have a pouch on my abdomen where I carry my babies for about three months until they are big enough to live in the outside world. When they are born, they are no bigger than a bumblebee."

Honeybee spoke up when he heard what Possum said about Bumblebee, "I don't know why any bee would want to live any other place on earth but here with all these pretty flowers just oozing nectar." Just to show he shared Bee's delight in the flowers, Hummingbird zipped over to feed from a cardinal flower. "It's not just the nectar I like", he said, "I also eat the small insects attracted to the blossoms."

Just then Squirrel poked her head out of the nesting box Thomas' granddad and grandmother had built. Having heard what Possum had said about carrying her babies in a pouch, Squirrel said, "Carrying her babies around in a pouch may be alright for Possum, but I'd rather leave mine in this box while I go out for a snack. I love to eat the acorns that grow on this tree my box is nailed to."

Snake was on the ground beneath the tree. He said, "I remember something I was told a long time ago. Thomas said his great-grand-father killed a snake in his hen house that had swallowed several eggs. After he pressed on the snake to retrieve the eggs, his great-grand-mother cooked them for breakfast." Does this whet your appetite?

DON'T KILL THAT SNAKE

Snakes are probably the world's most contradictory and maligned creatures. Loathed, loved, dreaded, admired, feared, worshiped, but never regarded indifferently, these fascinating reptiles are nature's paradox. They can swim gracefully without fins, climb agilely without feet, dig deeply without hands, and travel quickly without legs and with a body tightly packed in a sack like a sausage. In addition, they sleep with open lidless eyes, detect sounds though lacking outer ears, swallow food larger than they are, and, although often living on or under the ground, they are the cleanest of all animals.

The anatomy of a snake is unique. Lacking outer ears and eardrums, a snake has certain bones in the head that respond to sound waves and transmit them to the inner ear. The eyes, which never close, are covered by clear scales instead of eyelids. The two sides of a snake's jaw can be moved separately enabling it to swallow animals much larger than its own head. After downing a particularly large meal, with jaws askew, the snake simply yawns vigorously to snap them back in place.

The muscular arrangement which gives the body of a snake motion is among the most intricate in nature. With all his wisdom, Solomon confessed his inability to understand how a snake moves about when he spoke of "the way of a serpent upon a rock". The skin on the underside of a snake is a series of overlapping scales or plates. As a snake zigs his head first to one side and zags the body to the other, these plates catch irregularities on the surface on which the snake is crawling and shove it forward. This is the most common type of movement and is called "lateral undulation". In addition, a snake has at least three other gaits: a creeping "rectilinear movement" for climbing trees, a "concertina movement" for swinging through trees or smooth surfaces, and a "side-winding motion". The latter is the method of travel used by the small desert rattler called a "sidewinder". It travels over loose sand by jerky undulating motion, casting a loop ahead with the forepart of its body in order to get a grip against which to pull the remaining side-wise undulation forward.

BULL SNAKE

Although many snakes have dull camouflaging colors, other are striped, cross-banded, ringed, spotted, blotched, or speckled with beautiful hues of red, yellow, orange, pink, blue, green, brown or shiny black. One of the most colorful is the poisonous coral snake with its rings of yellow red, yellow black, in that order. Many harmless snakes have similar colors but none combines the characteristics of having the red and yellow rings in contact and the red continuing across the belly. There is a saying "red on yellow, kill a fellow".

Snakes are cold-blooded as their body temperature fluctuates with that of their immediate environment. A snake can be fully active only if the temperature ranges between 68 to 95 degrees. A temperature much over a 100 will kill it. It is progressively slowed as the temperature drops below its preferred range. In cold climates, snakes hibernate, usually underground, at which time the body temperature ranges from 39 to 41 degrees. Hundreds of snakes of various species may hibernate together if suitable sites are limited.

Some snakes lay eggs while others give live birth, with the majority of species in the United States reproducing by the former method. The cream-white eggs have a tough pliable covering which stretches as the snake develops. Most females leave the eggs as soon as they are laid, depending on the sun for incubating warmth. When ready to hatch, the young slash their way out of the shell with a special "egg tooth" that grows on the upper jaw. Having served its purpose, the tooth is shed soon after the snake emerges.

All snakes are carnivorous, feeding on such animals as groundhogs, rabbits, fish, frogs, lizards, worms, small birds, bird eggs, insects and other snakes. It is not necessary for them to feed frequently because they do not need food energy to maintain body heat as they remain inactive for long periods of time and have extensive tissues to store fat on which to subsist. They can go for weeks, months or even a year between meals.

Snakes have many enemies in addition to humans who kill them out of obsessive fear, as a sport when engaging in rattlesnake roundups, or for their meat and skins. Next to man, snakes themselves have been called their own worst enemy, often preying on one another. Other predators include eagles, owls, hawks, possums, skunks, deer, pigs, cats and dogs. Rodents often nibble on snakes that are sluggish from the cold, exposing them to fatal infections. In addition, automobiles and trains kill several million annually due to the reptile's habit of seeking the warmth radiating from pavement and steel tracks.

DIAMONDBACK RATTLESNAKE

Of some 250 species of snakes native to the United States, only four species are poisonous: rattlesnakes, copperheads, water moccasins and coral snakes. The first three are pit vipers possessing finely bored facial pits with fine membranes crammed with sensors that pick up infrared radiation from warm-blooded animals. Apparently used chiefly to direct the strike, the sensors can detect extremely small differences in temperature of its prey and the surroundings. Research done in 1936 by the Museum of Natural History in New York revealed that blindfolded snakes could still strike with accuracy at hot light bulbs.

North American poisonous snakes, although to be respected as dangerous, are not the killers many people assume. Snakes are timorous creatures who will slither out of the way when possible, often undetected. No American species will pursue a human. In an average year in the United States fewer than a dozen persons die from snake bites, less than fall victim to a bee sting. Over 90 percent of the cases reported of snake bite in the United States are "illegitimate", that is, sustained while deliberately handling or manipulating snakes.

Much of the fear with which people regard snakes is due to lack of knowledge about an animal that has been steeped in myth and superstition from early history. A few of the startling beliefs once held were that the earth grew from an egg hatched by an enormous snake, that earthquakes were caused by huge snakes moving around underground, and that a human could come back to life in the form of a snake to get revenge for the person who had been wronged. In addition to worshiping snakes, many people thought them to bring good luck, to have power over fertility of man, his beasts and his crops and to be able to cure illnesses. Even today, several religious cults in this country still use snakes extensively in their worship services. Of particular interest, the Hopi Indians of Arizona annually stage elaborate rain dances using snakes, believing that the reptiles will carry their prayers for rain to the gods who live underground.

One of the most widespread modern myths is that a snake can hypnotize its prey. Because they have no movable eyelids and can shift their eyes but very little, snakes tend to have a fixed stare. The "freeze" position assumed by the snake's intended victim is an attempt to escape notice and not a result of being hypnotized by the predator's gaze.

A prevalent misconception is that a snake must be coiled to strike, however a snake coiled in an S-shape can also thrust itself forward by straightening out the curves. A coiled snake can strike as much as two-thirds of its body length, but the distance is less from an uncoiled position. It has been observed that an automobile with the acceleration of a striking rattlesnake would go from zero to 60 miles an hour in half a second.

The myth that a rattlesnake will not crawl over a horsehair rope is thought to have originated as a joke perpetrated on newcomers by seasoned western cowboys. With a straight face, they would tell a tenderfoot to encircle the spot on the ground where he planned to sleep with a rope to prevent the dreaded rattlesnakes from entering the warm bed. The story was believed by so many that a newcomer could usually be spotted by the horsehair lariat attached to his saddle.

Since no animal lives by itself and for itself alone, a snake is a contributing member of the ecosystem in which it lives. An entirely different story is that of the Asian pythons introduced to Florida. They have no natural enemies there so it is up to man to try to eradicate them as they are causing so many problems, especially in the Everglades. Pythons are huge snakes as is illustrated by one captured weighing 104 pounds and another measuring 18 feet and 9 inches in length. While these pythons need to be banished, next time you see one of our native snakes, respect it and keep your distance if it is poisonous. And remember, don't kill that snake!

OTHER REPTILES

Lizards are the most abundant of all our reptiles in the United States. The majority of this species are land animals, but some are arboreal. Lizards eat insects and worms that they catch with their sticky tongues. They chew their food and lap up water with their tongues. The only poisonous lizard is the Gila monster of the southwestern United States, but there is a closely related species in Mexico. Lizards range in length from a few inches to 10 feet.

Some lizard species give live birth while others lay eggs. They deposit the eggs on the ground under   plants or among weeds and leave them to be incubated by the sun. The male sits on the female's back to fertilize eggs as they are laid. The eggs are laid in a long, string-like tube of gelatinous matter. Some species of lizards go into water only to lay their eggs, while others never leave the water. The green anole is one of my favorite lizard species.

Turtles and tortoises are separated by the places they occupy. Turtles are the marine or semi-aquatic form, while tortoises are terrestrial. There is a record of some sea turtles in Texas having to be rescued because of frigid temperatures as turtles are cold-blooded. Some turtles are called terrapins and have great commercial value.   The diamond-back terrapin of the Eastern seaboard is highly prized as a table delicacy. Even before World I, it was propagated on a large scale for human consumption.

Turtles swallow their food whole and drink by sucking. They have a short, broad body covered with a rigid shell into which the head and feet can be retracted. Eggs are shelled and usually laid in a cavity on the ground.

TURTLES ON A LOG

There are several animals classified as frogs. Bull frogs are aquatic, while tree frogs are arboreal. The tree frog has adhesive disks on its toes which permit it to climb trees. Horned toads are also called horned frogs and live on the ground.

The last reptiles I will cover in this chapter are fish. Fishermen seek certain species of fish that are enjoyed on the dinner table, often using minnows as bait. Tadpoles hatch from eggs laid in water and are the immature form of frogs. Many people stock small ponds with gold fish, tetra and Koi. Doing so can not only be a pleasure to observe, but the fish are a great means of mosquito control as these insects breed in water. One can use mosquito dunks in bird baths and other things containing water, but they are not necessary in a fish pond stocked with small fish.

HONEY IS THE BONUS

The incessant buzzing of bees is the song of a languid summer day. Insects of sunshine and fresh air, bees spend much of their lives collecting pollen and nectar for the production of honey, happily "doing what comes naturally" to the immense benefit of man and the environment.

Our language contains many colorful phrases using the word bee. Some familiar ones are spelling bee, husking bee, quilting bee, beeline, and busy as a bee. The word honeymoon comes from the old Germanic custom of couples drinking mead, a mixture made from fermented honey and water for a month after marriage.

Greek myth has a delightful explanation as to why some people have beautiful singing voices, others can deliver eloquent speeches, while still others write inspiring poetry. According to the myth, the muses, goddesses of arts and sciences, order a bee to place a drop of honey on the lips of these gifted individuals soon after they are born, thus imparting talent.

Honeybees were introduced to North America in 1638 when the pioneers, finding no native bees here, sent back to England for hives. The honeybees were called "white man's flies" by the Indians, who knew nothing of the sweetness of honey until escaping swarms of bees nested in the woods. Bees never become domesticated, those inhabiting a man-made hive can readily adjust to life in the wild as they are no different from a colony living in a tree.

While man's freight planes can carry a cargo of only about 25 percent of their weight, a bee can carry a load comparable to its own weight. The short, wide wings can beat in a weaving figure-8 motion as fast as 400 times a second, and fold instantly when the bee dives into a flower. When carrying a full cargo, a bee cruises at about 15 miles an hour. The fast-fanning wings are also used to air-condition the beehive by circulating air.

A bee colony normally consists of about 35,000 to 60,000 inhabitants most of which are undeveloped females classified as worker bees. These workers perform all the tasks of the hive except for the laying of eggs, which are produced by a single queen bee. In addition, a hive contains a few drones whose sole purpose in life is to mate with the queen and then they die.

HONEYBEES

In the wild, bees live in dark, secluded places such as hollow trees, logs, and old barns. Hunting for wild honey was once an important event for many families as honey was a major staple and honeycomb boiled down to beeswax was a basic ingredient in the production of candles which were used for lighting before electricity was available. To locate a bee tree, a small box was filled with honey and set outside. The bees would gorge on the honey and carry it back to their home. The searchers would then sight the direction of flight, thus establishing a "beeline". Then gradually they worked their way along the beeline, moving the honey box as they went and taking new sightings as necessary to extend the line until the honey site was located.

It was not until about 200 years ago that scientists discovered the value of bees as pollinators. They never gather nectar from but one species of flower on any one foraging trip. Going from blossom to blossom, the pollen that clings to the bee's hairy legs is transferred from one plant to another. They are unable to see the color red so red flowers must depend on other pollinators such as other insects and hummingbirds.

Some 90 crops of the United States are dependent on insect pollination, primarily performed by honeybees. From an economic standpoint, a colony of bees is worth 20 to 40 times as much in the pollination of crops as in the production of honey and beeswax. The majority of the roughly 1,000,000 colonies of bees used commercially for pollination are utilized in alfalfa fields and almond and apple orchards. They are also used regularly for pollination of ornamental plants and some forest plants on which birds and other wildlife depend on for food. In addition, bees are used to pollinate such crops as blueberries, cantaloupes, clovers, vetch, cherries, prunes, plums, cranberries, cucumbers and watermelons.

One bee could never make a pound of honey in its lifetime. It would have to visit a million flowers a day and fly a distance equal to two complete trips around the world to gather enough nectar. The sweet bonus of the bees could not be ours to enjoy were not these insects as cooperative as they are industrious. The soothing buzz of a peaceful summer song reassures that flowers will bloom, forests will thrive, crops will prosper, and honey will grace our tables.

SLY AS A FOX

In Aesop's fable "The Fox and the Grapes", the story goes like this. One day Fox spotted a beautiful bunch of grapes hanging from a vine on a tree. They looked ripe and his mouth began to water as he gazed at them. The grapes were up high so Fox had to jump to try to reach them. After trying over and over again without success, he walked away with his nose in the air saying, "I'm sure they are sour". From this fable arose the expression "sour grapes" used when we can't get what we would like to have. Actually, I've read that grapes and several other fruits are toxic to foxes, dogs and some other canines.

There's another fable that is entitled "The Fox and the Crow". One bright morning Fox was following his sharp nose in search of something to eat. He saw Crow on a limb of an overhead tree. Crow had found a piece of cheese and flew to a branch to eat it. Fox, wanting the cheese for himself, flattered the crow, calling him beautiful and asking if the crow's voice was equally sweet. When Crow let out a loud "caw" he dropped the cheese and Fox devoured it.

Coyotes, wolves, jackals, dogs and foxes are all in the Canidae family of animals. The first four listed are of the genus Canus, but the fox is of the Vulpes genus. There are many sayings referring to various animals. In addition to "wise as an owl" and "sly as a fox", some others are "strong as an ox", "blind as a bat", "slippery as an eel", "sick as a dog", "crazy as a loon", and, although not about an animal, there's "hard as a rock", and "thin as a rail". Challenge your memory and add some more.

GRAY FOX

Foxes are nocturnal and usually solitary. They have slight build, short legs, long bushy tails and usually long ears. Their intelligence and cunning are proverbial, and their senses are remarkably acute. They eat mostly mice, rats, insects and worms. They will occasionally attack lambs and fawns, especially when extra food is required to feed numerous cubs. As noted in Aesop's fable, they are fond of fruit. The common red fox is widely distributed over North America, while the gray fox appears only in the southern region. The smallest of our foxes is the kit fox that is an inhabitant of the Southwestern states.

In 2021, a judge ordered the federal government to come up with a plan to release more endangered red wolves from breeding programs to bolster the dwindling wild populations. At the time, there were as few as seven wild wolves and they are on the endangered species list. They were to be released in North Carolina, the only place in the world where this wolf roams wild outside of zoos and wildlife refuges.

POLLINATION

Pollinators are animals that transfer pollen from one plant to another. They are essential in the production of many crops and wildflowers. The honeybee is recognized as the most important, but bumblebees and other solitary bees, butterflies, moths, flies, hummingbirds, bats, and even beetles are also pollinators. Some plants such as corn and tomatoes rely on wind for pollination. That is why farmers and home gardeners plant a few rows side by side for better pollination. When you see an ear of corn that does not have kernels covering the entire cob, it did not have sufficient pollination.

North America alone is home to over 4,000 native bees that vary in size from the tiny perdits to the large carpenter and bumblebees. The coloration of bees may be striped yellow, orange or red; others range in color from all black to metallic blue and green.

Providing habitat around your home to support our six-legged friends will benefit more than just pollinators as healthy gardens support many other insects. Among those recognized as natural enemies of garden pests are green lacewings, ladybugs, spiders, and solitary wasps which take care of the pests without the need to spray pesticides. Avoid the use of pesticides as they will destroy your pollinators along with the bad guys.

Poet Ogden Nash once penned, "My garden will never make me famous. I'm a horticultural ignoramous". I agree with him as I'm still learning things about horticulture. I've been known to say that every time I think I know everything, I learn something new. Maybe an old dog can be taught a few new tricks.

HONEYBEE IN A TREE CAVITY

Bees collect pollen to feed their young while butterflies search for host plants on which to lay their eggs. Both pollinate plants as they zip from blossom to blossom. Not all plants are equal in producing pollen and nectar so a garden should be planned to have a good source of both throughout the year. I have a bulletin that states: bee diverse, bee native, bee patient, bee gentle, bee chemical free, bee friendly, bee a little messy, bee aware, and bee sunny.

Some good plants to supply both nectar and pollen are spring-flowering bulbs, azaleas, zinnias, salvias, milkweeds, dandelions, sedums, lavender, mistflowers, partridge peas, blackberry, grapes, plums, apples, asters, sunflowers, goldenrods, thistles, ironweeds, violas, pansies, and dianthus. You will notice that this list includes plants that bloom in late winter, spring, summer, fall, and those that blossom throughout the winter. Happy pollinator gardening!

BATS ON PATROL

Bats are mosquito-chomping champs. They are even better than purple martins and other swallows that feed on insects as they fly about. The reason bats are the champs is that as mosquitos become more active late in the evening and at night, so do bats. While swallows are snoozing, the bats are out on patrol.

Bats maneuver with the assistance of a membrane between the tail and hind limbs. The thumb claws extend slightly ahead of the wings stretched between the elongated digits of the hand. The membrane between the tail and the hind limbs aids the bat as it flies about scooping up insects.

Bats have large ears. Flying bats, even if blinded, can detect obstacles in their path by emitting supersonic notes so high pitched that they cannot be heard by humans. Like a radar, they can determine the location of the reflected sound and thus avoid the obstacles.

BIG BROWN BAT

Bats are widely distributed in temperate and tropical regions. The largest of all bats are the "great flying foxes" of Malaysia that weigh two pounds and have a wingspread of five feet.

In the winter, bats in large numbers congregate in caves to hibernate. The presence of so many close together helps keep them warm. Some species choose to migrate south for the winter. The little brown bat sets the record for length of hibernation. It hibernates for six months in barns, hollow trees or attics.

If you purchase or build a bat house, it should be mounted at least 10 to 15 feet high on a tree or wall. It is best to face the house south or east and place it so it will get several hours of morning sun. With bats on patrol, you might be able to throw away those mosquito dunks you have been putting in bird baths and other things that hold water.

COLORS OF THE SEASONS

According to the artist, John Ruskin, "Nature is painting for us, day after day, pictures of infinite beauty". This quote reminds me of something that happened many years ago. I was out in her yard with one of my cousins, viewing all the beautiful flowers and enjoying the singing birds. Her three-year-old granddaughter was also present. When my cousin told the little girl that God made all these wonderful things for us to enjoy, the child exclaimed, "Didn't Him do a good job!". I think that we will all agree that Him did a good job in providing these treasures of nature to enthrall us.

There is a story that an old forecaster said that he was looking for the acknowledged king of predictions to forecast what kind of winter to expect. According to him, the king is the wooly bear, a moth caterpillar. The wooly bear starts stirring in the fall and if you see a lot of them, it means a hard winter is coming. Also if their coat is heavy, a hard winter is predicted. The old forecaster added that you can also predict the kind of winter coming by looking at dogwoods, hollys and hickorys. If they set heavy fruit, you can expect a hard winter.

Color begins in our gardens in late winter as plants produced by bulbs begin to bloom. The first to bloom is the paper-white which often begins blooming in late December. Once someone accidentally spilled an alcoholic beverage into a pot of paper-whites causing them to shorten and not flop over. For these imbibers, use nine parts of water to one part of alcohol. Use rum, gin, tequila or vodka, but no beer or wine.

Daffodils (narcissus) may be white, yellow, red, orange or pink. Many have a sweet scent. Some think that leucojums are narcissus but they are a different genus. Their blooms are white with green dots near tips of blossoms. They are often called spring snowflake and summer snowflake, even though it blooms in spring.

Alliums include onions, leeks and chives. They bloom from spring to late summer in colors of white, bright blue or purple. Amaryllis blooms from early spring to late fall with pink blossoms. Anemones bloom spring to early fall, although there are more in bloom in spring. Colors are white, blue, pink, magenta, crimson, red, violet, lavender, yellow and even green. Lilies bloom from early summer to late fall and may be of almost any color. An added plus is the sweet scent of many lilies.

Demur garden club ladies call them "magic", "resurrection", or "surprise" lilies, but the rest of us know them as "naked ladies". You might call them surprise lilies as that's what they do when they suddenly pop up out of the ground in mid-summer with no foliage on the stems.

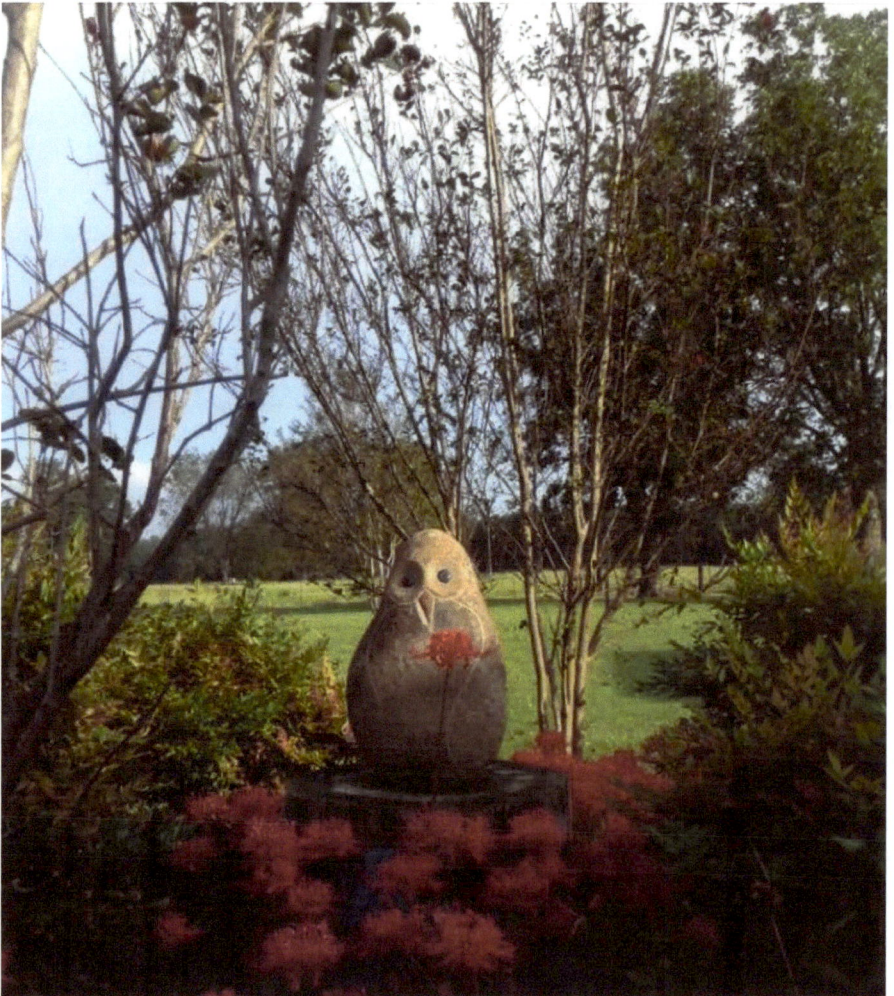

SPIDER LILIES

Another plant of the Lycoris genus is the spider lily that appears in September or October with bright red blooms. Both lilies of this genus put on foliage after blooming. Growing spider lilies in your lawn causes no problems as they will have stored food for next fall's surprise party by the time mowing is needed in the spring. There is another plant of a different genus called spider lily that appears in wet areas in the southern states. It produces white blooms in springtime.

In fall, the leaves of many deciduous trees and shrubs become colorful. Various colors may be yellow, orange, red, purple or a combination of more than one color. The green pigment in the leaves starts to deteriorate. If sugars and starches have accumulated in the leaves by the time the chlorophyll (green pigment) disappears, there's a good probability that we can see those beautiful colors in our own yards. Later the leaves fall from the tree and become a valuable mulch beneath the tree and later decay to be a sponge to conserve water for future use by the tree.

COLORFUL FALL FOLIAGE

Many people plan a fall trip to the northeastern states in the fall to view the beautiful fall foliage usually abundant there. The above photograph was taken on such a trip. However, in many years we have beautiful foliage of various colors in the southern states. The most colorful in my yard are a red maple, sumacs, plums, redbuds and Virginia creeper.

THE PIONEERS' WONDER TREE

Today sassafras is just another unknown tree in the woods for many people, but in early colonial times it was commonly sought as a wonderful-tasting, pleasant-smelling cure-all.

Dr. Nicholas Monardes wrote in 1577 that an extract from sassafras bark and roots could cure most ills; that it was a remedy for "large importune fevers", "griefs of the breast caused by cold humours" and "griefs of the head". He believed that it was good for "them that be lame and creepelles and them that are not able to goe", and that it "comforteth the liver and stomacke".

Sassafras albidum, a member of the laurel family of plants, is the only species of its genus found in North America. Only two other species exist in the world, one native to the island of Taiwan and the other in the mainland of China.

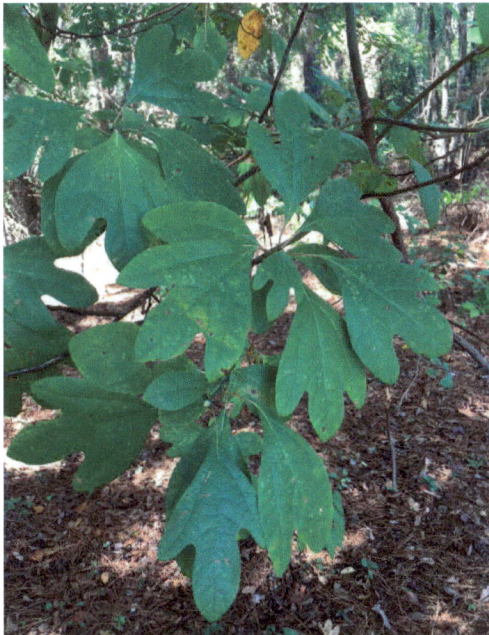

SASSAFRAS

The leaves, twigs, and bark of sassafras are all spicy aromatic. Another unique characteristic is the multiple leaf shapes. The four different shapes are likely to appear on the same tree, even on the same branch. The light green leaves may take an oval shape, right-hand mitten shape, left-hand mitten shape or be three-lobed.

The yellow-orange and blood-red iridescence of sassafras brightens the forest in late summer when the leaves begin to change color. At this time the tree's fruit appears as dark blue drupes at the tips of the red stems. Unsuitable for human consumption, the fruits are relished by songbirds, bobwhites, wild turkey and black bears, while the twigs are browsed by rabbits and whitetail deer.

Although sassafras commonly reaches a height of only about 20 feet, there are records of trees exceeding 50 feet in height and 3 feet in diameter. The soft, light brown wood is used for posts, barrels, small boats and siding for houses.

Early American pioneers, convinced that anything as odorous as sassafras must be a good insect repellent, built bedsteads of the wood to keep away bedbugs, constructed hen houses of sassafras to repel chicken lice and sometimes laid floors in their houses of the aromatic wood to prevent insect problems. Had sassafras possessed the powers the pioneers attributed to it, modern chemical pest control businesses would have never flourished.

Many superstitions were associated with sassafras by early Americans. Boring of the wood was considered bad luck by some New Englanders, and in the Ozarks if sassafras popped while burning, it was an omen of death. Housewives in Kentucky used a ladle made of sassafras for stirring when making lye soap, believing the soap would not turn out well with the use of any other wood.

As news of the wonder tree spread to Europe in early colonial times, expeditions to America eagerly sought sassafras. Worth 336 pounds sterling per ton in Britain, a load of sassafras root could determine the success of a voyage. Although the popularity of sassafras quickly diminished in Europe, it was still lauded as a spring tonic "to thin the blood" and was used to treat colds, fevers and rheumatic pains.

As the years passed, however, the use of sassafras as a medicine waned and even a suspicion that it can be harmful has been aroused. Records proved that it caused cancer in laboratory test animals. By the nineteenth century, what had been hailed as the pioneers' panacea began to be used in other ways. Sassafras became popular as flavor for candies, medicines and drinks. Sarsaparilla, the soft drink ordered in saloons by the "good guys" in the old western movies, used oil of sassafras as does root beer. The oil is also used to perfume soap.

Louisiana Cajuns introduced the use of powered leaves of sassafras to thicken and flavor soups, gumbo and various creole dishes. The spice, labeled "File" in grocery stores, can be easily prepared at home by drying leaves and crushing them. You will readily become aware of the thickening and flavoring qualities if you pick a green leaf and chew it for a few seconds.

While sassafras may not comfort the liver nor keep the hen house pest-free, it does have many modern uses. Think about the pioneers' wonder tree with the multiple leaf shapes and aromatic scent next time you sip a frosted root beer or savor a piping hot bowl of filet gumbo.

THAT WHICH WE CALL A ROSE

Do you think that horsetail, cranesbill, catclaw, hound's tongue, lizard's tail, goats beard, and goat head refer to anatomical parts of animals? Not exclusively. All are common names for plants of widespread distribution and elude to a resemblance of some part of the plant to the object for which the plant is named.

Some plants have a dozen or more different common names as is illustrated by Houstonia. This genus is known as bluets, Quaker ladies, Quaker bonnets, star-violet, little washerwoman, blue-eyed babies, wild forget-me-not, eye-bright, angel eyes, nuns, innocents, star of Bethlehem, and Venus' pride. In other instances, the same name is applied to any number of totally unrelated plants. Bluebell can be any of the following: a perennial shrub, a freely climbing more or less herbaceous vine, an annual herb, or several species of the bluebell family.

Because of the perplexity of common names, scientific names are necessary to eliminate confusion. But despite their limitations, common names are still preferred by many lay people for their simplicity and often their descriptiveness. Some names can be poetic, charming, suggestive, puzzling, or even downright deceptive. In some cases one is left to wonder why a particular name has become associated with a plant, but even though many are misnomers, names of longstanding become those plants to which they refer. Shakespeare's Juliet said, "That which we call a rose, by any other name would smell as sweet". But consider the aesthetic adjustment if rose were changed to ragweed, lilac to lousewort or holly to horse nettle. Four hundred years later, a rose is still a rose even as Romeo remained a Montague.

Abraham Lincoln once said, "We can complain because roses have thorns, or rejoice because thorn bushes have roses". However, not all rose bushes have thorns. The Zephirine Drouhin rose has no thorns, will prosper in either sun or shade, blooms almost continuously and has a pleasing aroma.

ROSE BUSH IN BLOOM

Some plants have names so descriptive of obvious physical characteristics that an explanation of the origin would be superfluous. Anyone familiar with such plants as bitterweed, lady's slipper, shooting star, goldenrod, cat-tail, blazing star, Indian paintbrush, black-eyed Susan, devil's walking stick, trumpet vine, elephant's ear or coneflower, to name but a few, would not question their nomenclature. Space here will be devoted to brief explanations of what is commonly believed to be the origins of a few interesting plant names.

TOUCH-ME-NOT: when touched, the dried seed pods split and explosively cast seeds in all directions.

BLOOD ROOT: the horizontal rootstock is a fleshy rhizome containing blood-red juice used by the Indians for dye.

BLACKBERRY LILY: shiny black seeds closely resemble blackberries.

DUTCHMAN'S BRITCHES: the flower "britches" hang upside down, being attached at the crotch to a stem.

ST. ANDREW'S CROSS: four yellow petals aligned in an X-shape like the St. Andrew's cross.

JACOB'S LADDER: ladder-like arrangement of the leaflets.

SKULLCAP: seeds shaped like a skull cap.

BEARD'S TONGUE: rather than producing pollen, one of the five stamens is modified into a hairy "tongue", probably to attract insects.

MILFOIL: this word of French origin means "a thousand leaves".

IRONWEED: refers to the hardness and stiffness of the stems.

GREEN DRAGON: segments of deeply divided leaves resemble dragon's claws.

CRANEBILL: seedpods form sharply-pointed "cranes' bills".

HOUND'S TONGUE: descriptive of large, soft, floppy leaves.

EVENING PRIMROSE: the flowers, which depend on night flying moths to pollinate, open very suddenly, with the movement being visible, in late afternoon and close the following morning if the day is sunny.

SOAPWORT: contains a mucilaginous sap which forms lather in water.

ROSIN WEED: contains a resinous sap.

CATCHFLY: has a sticky substance on stems which traps insects.

SNEEZE WEED: powdered disk flowers, once used as snuff, cause violent sneezing.

HONEY LOCUST: seed pods contain a thin, sweet, honey-like pulp.

SMARTWEED: no smarter than a "dumb cane" (dieffenbachia). Crystals in smartweed are peppery and smart the tongue or skin. Those in dumb cane have a numbing effect.

HOP TREE: the unripe seeds have been substituted for hops in making beer.

NEW JERSEY TEA: a tea which does not contain caffeine was first brewed from the leaves during the American Revolution.

HENBIT: constitutes a "bit for the hen" as it is eaten by both wild and domestic birds.

SELF-HEAL or HEAL-ALL: widespread belief in its healing powers for numerous ailments.

BONESET: used in early times to supposedly dull pain when setting bones.

DAIZY FLEABANE: dried flower heads were believed to repel fleas.

RATTELSNAKE-MASTER: early American folklore attributed medical properties to the juice of this plant as a remedy for rattlesnake bites.

SCOURING RUSH or HORSETAIL: plant has high mineral content with abrasive action. You might try polishing an old penny to check it out. The alternative name refers to the appearance, which is that of a horse's tail neatly tied.

COMPASS PLANT: the edges of the lower leaves are turned north and south when growing in full sun.

JUDAS TREE: a redbud, which according to legend was the kind of tree from which Judas hanged himself.

FROSTWEED: contorted ice shapes, or "frost flowers", are formed when water is forced through cracks just above the roots during the first severe freeze of the winter.

CENTURY PLANT: the name is misleading as the plant blooms once, after 8 to 10 years of life, not 100.

SENSITIVE PLANT: the leaves are touch-sensitive, closing upward against each other when pressed. This action is a result of pressure exerted from within the cell walls by the cell contents.

SUNFLOWER: the flowers turn to follow the sun.

OBEDIENT PLANT: flowers can be pushed right or left and they will remain in the position to which they are turned.

And a rose is called a rose simply because, the opinion of Shakespeare's Juliet notwithstanding, by no other name would it smell as sweet.

PLEASE PASS THE SMILAX

"What was your favorite subject?", Jimmy asked David as the two eleven-year-old boys rode in the back seat of a car as David's dad was driving them home from Ecology Camp. "It was all fun stuff, but I guess I liked aquatic biology best. Getting to wade in the water was cool." Jimmy twisted David's meaning. "Not just cool. Freezing! At the eight o'clock class I was so cold I couldn't hardly move."

"The only thing about aquatics I didn't like was the leeches. I only got one on me, but Brad found three stuck on him when he changed from his wet shorts after class.", David grimaced, remembering the loathsome little creatures. "Yuck! Did they suck all his blood dry like a vampire bat?" The boys laughed loudly, apparently finding this remark hilarious.

Shortly David recovered enough to speak. "I had a hard time telling which was a mayfly and which was a dragonfly. Did you?" "Not if they were resting. Our instructor Eddis said a mayfly always holds its wings in a vertical position and a dragonfly holds them horizontal."

After a brief pause, David asked, "What was your favorite subject?" "I liked botany. We got to eat all the plants and stuff." "Yeah, I liked that, too. And when we went up on the mountain on our way to Freeman's Valley, we ate bunches of blueberries all along the way."

"Freeman's Valley was awesome! I liked standing under those big umbrella magnolia leaves. I bet they really could keep the rain off. The cinnamon ferns were cool, too. They were taller than I was." "Yeah, they were taller than me, too. They were even as tall as our instructor Clifford and I'll bet he's six feet." "I wish we could've been at camp when Freeman Thomas was teaching botany." "Yeah. The kids must have liked him a lot to name a valley after him. But I like Clifford, too."

SMILAX

"Did you like chewing the sassafras leaves, David?" "Sorta. It was kinda yucky, but I just kept chewing and my spit got thicker and thicker." "When I get home, I'm gonna pick some for Mom to put in her gumbo. Clifford says that's what thickens it." "But you gotta dry them and smush'em up", reminded David. "I really liked eating the tender little shoots of smilax", Jimmy remembered. "Me, too. Clifford said they tasted just like asparagus, but I dunno, I never eat that pukey green stuff." "Me neither. One day in botany class we named all the things we could think of that plants are good for. Did you get to do that?" "Yeah", answered David.

"Let's take turns doing that now. You go first", suggested Jimmy. The things the two boys named were food, clothes, houses, lumber, supply oxygen, medicine, furniture, shade, air-conditioning (referring to a tree's cooling through transpiration), look pretty, absorb noise, clean the air by taking up carbon dioxide, homes for animals, food for animals, and prevent the soil from washing away. In one group, after a lengthy listing, one highly impressed little girl exclaimed, "Without plants, we'd all be dead and there'd be nothing to bury us in!".

Following a stop at a gas station, the boys clambered back into the car. Within moments, they were back on the subject of activities at the camp. Sponsored by the Arkansas Audubon Society and held the second week of June each year at Camp Clearfork on the Ouachita River in Arkansas, the camp is for boys and girls eleven and twelve years of age. The top twelve students are invited back for a second year of instruction.

"I got up every morning but one to go on the early morning bird walk", bragged Jimmy. "I just went twice but I got to see the American redstart Robin caught in the mist net. She said it was the neatest bird she'd ever caught." "I liked ornithology, but sometimes it was dumb when we couldn't find any birds", said Jimmy. "I found a bird at the edge of the water that nobody else got to see", boasted David. "Even Robin couldn't locate it at first, but then she asked me to describe it and tell her what it was doing. When I told her it was doing pushups, she said it was a waterthrush". Robin had tentatively identified the bird by the field marks David had listed and by the fact that it was at the water's edge, but the clincher had been the boy's unique description of a waterthrush's peculiar bobbing habit.

"Did you get to see the owl pellets?", asked Jimmy. "Yeah, all those bones and fur and hair and stuff they can't digest so they throw'em back up". "I'd puke too if I ate rats and mice!". The two boys collapsed in boisterous guffaws at Jimmy's crude remark. David's dad had to ask them to "tone it down a bit back there."

A subdued David resumed the conversation. "The evening programs were mostly okay. I really liked Jane Gulley's with the eagles, hawks and owls." "Those dumb girls sitting in front of us thought an owl could turn its head completely around", derided Jimmy, snug in his male superiority. "I sure knew better. I read about owls all the time in the Ranger Rick magazine. I know that owls can turn their heads only about 270 degrees in either direction. They have to be able to do this because their eyes won't move in their sockets", stated David.

"I sure liked running around with those insect nets in entomology", Jimmy recalled. "Yeah, I kinda like insects except chiggers and mosquitos and fleas and spiders". "Dummy! Spiders aren't insects", scoffed Jimmy. "I know that, stupid! But we did study about them in entomology. I know that spiders have eight legs and insects have only six". "And we're supposed to like spiders because Susan says they keep a lot of pest insects in check", stated Jimmy.

"Well, I betcha Michelle doesn't like brown recluses!", exclaimed David. "But they said they didn't think the bite she got was gonna be as bad as the one Freeman got several years ago". "I bet that's why he doesn't come back to camp anymore", offered David. While Freeman does still have a large scar on his arm where the flesh rotted away, the spider bite would not have prevented his returning to the camp he loves. He now calls himself "retired from camp teaching", making room for younger instructors.

"Cabins full of brown recluses sure wouldn't keep me away. I sure hope I get invited back next year". "Me too. Camp was awesome. Even the brown recluses and the leeches and the poison ivy", David said, scratching the angry rash on his ankles.

A LOUISIANA COTTAGE GARDEN

If you turned onto my street from Highway 79 last summer you were greeted by a panorama of colorful blossoms replacing much of the lawn in front of my house. Gone also were the shrubs that stood like somber sentinels guarding the foundation but adding little to the aesthetic impact.

The English have always favored "cottage gardens" in which a medley of annual and perennial flowers grow in a jumbled confusion of color in front of their homes. Most Americans, in contrast, pride themselves on meticulously groomed lawns with sculptured shrubs near their houses. Flowers, if used at all, are relegated to very narrow strips.

In the last several years a few pioneering gardeners have dared to flaunt tradition and last spring it was my decision to join them. Out came the shrubs, up came much of the lawn and a Louisiana cottage garden was in the making. Its area swings out in flowing curves for about 25 feet all across the front of my house.

Pull into one of the parking bays bordered by an expanse of yellow lantanas and I'll give you a personal tour. By late May my garden had already become a haven for butterflies, hummingbirds, toads, lizards, box turtles, and bumblebees as well as a host of other beneficial insects. Narrow paths of pine straw snake among the plants giving access for grooming the flowers or getting a closeup view.

A bird bath in the shade of a large yaupon and a feeder mounted on a redwood post amid the globe amaranth invite the birds to add their visual, as well as audible, appeal. Their impressive numbers could be in response to a message on a weathered gray board which proclaims, "EVERY BIRDIE WELCOME".

Several species of butterflies float over the buddleia, cleome, zinnias, marigolds, and lantana, while the salvia seems to be preferred by the bumblebees. So profuse are their numbers that my children have dubbed the area "Mother's bumblebee garden". Because of the myriad of plant species available, other beneficial insects are also attracted to the garden.

Four chairs are grouped in pairs under two of the tulip poplars in front of the planting bed. Pull up a chair and we'll enjoy a refreshing glass of lemonade while we watch the hummingbirds hovering over the blossoms or darting at each other around the hanging feeder. Orchard orioles also frequent this feeder, announcing their arrival with a raspy chatter.

COTTAGE GARDEN

Luscious rose-colored mandevilla blossoms ornament a black iron arch placed between windows near the center of the front wall of the house. Beneath the arch are pink and blue veronicas, another of the plants favored by butterflies. To the right of the arch is a Victorian rose pillar, its occupant a Zephirine Drouhin thorn-free rose which has cerise-pink blooms with a delicious fragrance.

Now that it is late winter, if you stop by for a visit you may not be dramatically impressed with my cottage garden, its main focal points a red osier dogwood and two heavily-berried yaupon shrubs often frequented by hungry birds. But the visionary will recognize the precocious yellow daffodils as heralds for the many perennials in restless sleep beneath their blanket of mulched leaves.

BREAKFAST IS SERVED

The early rays of the sun sparkled on the gossamer web stretched from the coral honeysuckle trellis to the camelia bush. Charlotte was in her lair, awaiting the unwary prey which would provide her with breakfast. My own morning repast, two blueberry muffins and a generous glass of orange juice, which I was enjoying on the patio, had been more easily obtained than Charlotte's. A tiny cottontail rabbit hopped from beneath the ligustrum hedge not 20 feet from the table where I sat. Probably only recently weaned by his mother, he was not yet wary of human presence. Breakfast for him consisted of the greening blades of the early-April grass. He wrinkled his pink nose and pulsated his tiny cheeks rapidly as he nibbled.

ROBINS IN A TREE

An enthusiastic robin probing in a freshly-dug flower bed was reaping the rewards of the proverbial early bird. As she pulled a fat earthworm from the soil, another robin came eagerly hopping over, imploring her to share. The young bird opened its beak widely and shivered its wings in anticipation. What's a mother to do? Postponing her own breakfast, she poked the tasty morsel in her offspring's gaping mouth.

The tiny bluebirds in the nesting box were having breakfast in bed as usual. Although both parents were engaged in providing room service, hers was the more dedicated effort. Much of his time was spent atop the birdhouse warbling his muted song. If it were a lullaby he sang, it was ineffectual, as the ravenous babies never ceased their clamor for nourishment.

As I finished my breakfast by giving the remaining crumbs of the muffins to a Carolina wren out searching for minute insects in the potted geraniums, I noticed the spider still motionless in the center of her web. But even as I watched, a deer fly zoomed into the sticky filament and became hopelessly entangled. With a pounce, Charlotte had her delayed breakfast.

GOLDEN SEEDS SOWN UPON THE NIGHT

In poetic expression, James Russell Lowell penned, "The firefly twinkles, His fitful heat-lightnings". But there is no heat involved in the gleaming flashes. The most efficient light known today is the "cold" light from the flicker of a firefly. Its organic luminescence produces only light, with none of its energy wasted generating heat. In comparison, electricity produces about 10 percent light and 90 percent heat, while the sun gives off about 35 percent light with 65 percent heat.

Fireflies, sometimes called lightning bugs, are not flies at all, but are small to medium sized, soft-bodied, dark-colored beetles. There are over 2,000 species worldwide, with over 100 native to North America. The specimen most likely to be captured in the South by a youngster engaging in the perennial summer sport of catching lightning bugs in a jar is a species that flies low and slow.

In many species of fireflies, the eggs, larvae and pupae are all luminescent, although they are not as brilliant as adult fireflies. The firefly larvae and also the wingless, grub-like adult females of some species are called glowworms.

Cuban women sometimes wear a large species of firefly called a click beetle as ornamentation on their ball gowns or in nets in their hair. These beetles give off a strong green light and with any movement, such as dancing, glow even more brilliant until no glittering diamond can compete. The click beetles are also used as lanterns by placing a large number in a bottle. Although individually they admit their light in flashes, together they give continuous, though wavering, light. Men walking through dense tropical forests at night often attach fireflies to their boots to light the path ahead.

Two of the rare chemicals contained in the bodies of fireflies, lucifein and luciferase, are used extensively in cancer research and other significant experiments. The Sigma Firefly Scientists Club is an organization whose purpose is to supply fireflies to scientists all over the world for research.

Dr. James Lloyd of the University of Florida, who has spent nearly two decades studying the behavior of fireflies, offers some tips for conducting your own experiments on a warm summer evening. Dr. Lloyd suggests that you arm yourself with a penlight and locate a lawn full of fireflies. Your target should be a male of a species that generally moves across the lawn emitting its characteristic one-half-second flash every five to seven seconds. Use your penlight to imitate the female which rarely flies but usually responds from her perch on a blade of grass. When she sees the male's signal, she waits two seconds and flashes a single response. Keep aiming your penlight toward the male and answer each flash. As the male nears, answer his flash promptly without the usual two-second delay. He is likely to hesitate, but will probably flash again. If you continue flashing without delay, he will fly away believing the responses to be from a female of another species.

It's well to be wary as fireflies are sometimes cannibalistic. The male Photinus pyralis is often victimized by the larger, aggressive female of another genus. His romantic midsummer night's dream often becomes a nightmare as he alights and is devoured by a female more interested in lunch than love.

Fireflies have captivated children throughout the ages and these fascinating insects have inspired many poets. A century ago James Whitcomb Riley wrote "The fireflies, like golden seeds, are sown upon the night". And for every summer to come, a warm summer night will find children attempting to harvest some of these glimmering seeds in a glass jar, not understanding the complex scientific explanation of the rhythmic glowing, but simply delighting in the mysteries of nature.

HABITATS OF PLANTS AND ANIMALS

Many plants and animals are very selective about their habitats, while others are not so picky-picky. There are so many plants that grow in and by water that I will only list a few of them here: water lily, water lotus, scouring rush, frogbit, algae, parrots feather, water lettuce, water hyacinth, cattail, iris, pondweed, and duckweed.

WATER LILIES

Likewise, there are many animals that live in the water, some of which never leave it while others go ashore. Ducks, geese, and pelicans usually feed in the water, while others like gulls, terns and several other species of shorebirds feed mostly on shore. Fish, some frogs, trapdoor snails, water moccasins and some other water-dwelling snakes, never leave the water.

Some plants and animals live in deserts and other arid areas. Mesquite and cacti both are adapted to arid sites. In 1901, the bluebonnet won as the Texas State Flower. Other contenders were the cotton boll and the prickly pear cactus. "Cactus Jack" Nance Garner lobbied for the cactus bloom. Cacti do have beautiful blooms when they put on a show in rainy weather, but my family and I surely enjoy the beauty of bluebonnets that blanket the roadsides on spring trips to Texas. Two of my sons own small ranches in Texas, with many bluebonnets on their land. One time an aunt was visiting one of them and the two went out for a walk. He warned her that she was stepping on his bluebonnets, but the plants were so plentiful that there was no place else to put a foot.

BARREL CACTUS

114

West Texas is home to plants like cacti and mesquite, which thrive under dry conditions. Also, there are several animals like rattlesnakes and gila monsters that favor arid sites. There are even animals that live underground, such as burrowing owls, badgers, ground squirrels, moles, ground hogs, and earth worms.

Animals that live in trees include squirrels, birds, tree frogs and some snakes. Then there are plants that can be found in shady areas of dense woods. Lichens, cross vines, mistletoe, mayapples, toadstools and moss, all prosper in wooded areas.

MAYAPPLE

Many birds migrate with the changing of the seasons. Those nesting in the northern states come down to become our winter guests here in the south. They may include juncos, white-throated and white-crowned sparrows, purple finches, gold finches and pine siskins. Other species just pass through on their routes to the south in the fall and north in the spring. A few four-footed animals also engage in migration, some just moving up or down a mountain in order to find a good food supply as the seasons change. It is desirable to have berry-producing trees and shrubs and filled feeders for your avian guests.

SOME CHARACTERISTICS OF BIRDS

There are many references to what groups of birds are called. I'll list many of them here: a murder of crows, rookery of albatross, colony of auks, a colony of avocets, a crowd of blackbirds, wake of buzzards, raft of coots, herd of cranes, bevy of doves, paddling of ducks, congress of eagles (I wonder if they are Democrats or Republicans), soar of falcons, gaggle of geese, colony of gulls, kettle of hawks, band or scald of blue jays, wisdom of owls, covey of quail, loft of pigeons, breast of robins, and a host of sparrows. And unfortunately too many of the imported house sparrows.

There are at least 40 colors used in the names of birds. Black occurs 38 times, white 30, red 26, yellow 18, blue 13, and gray also 13 times. The other colors occur far fewer times than these six colors I've listed.

Our largest bird is the California condor which measures 45 inches in length and 120 in wingspread. The white pelican comes in a close second, being 5 inches longer, but 10 inches less in wingspread. Other large birds are swans which measure up to 95 inches in length, whooping cranes are 45 inches in length and have a wingspread of 90 inches, the Laysan albatross is 28 inches long with a wingspread of 80 inches, bald eagles are 32 inches in length and have a wingspread of 80, turkey vultures are 25 inches long with a wingspread of 72 inches, and great white herons measure 38 inches in length and their wingspread is 70 inches. When I typed the word pelican above, I thought of a saying about this bird. It goes, "The pelican, its beak can hold more than its belly can". Quite likely true.

There are several small owls, among them the elf which is five and one-fourth inches long with a wingspread of fifteen inches and the pygmy owl which is 6 inches long and has a wingspread of 15 inches. Our largest woodpecker is the ivory-billed which has now been declared extinct in North America. Now our largest is the pileated woodpecker. Our flycatcher with the longest tail is the scissor-tailed. Our smallest bird is the calliope hummingbird which is two and one-fourth inches long.

There are some birds named for what they seem to be saying when they sing or call. Among them are bobwhite, chickadee, chuck-will's-widow, and whip-poor-will. Mourning doves appear to be expressing sorrow when they call. Mute swans might as well have lost their voices as all they utter is a low grunt that is rarely audible. The whistling swan's call is a musical whistle, while that of the trumpeter swan is a low-pitched trumpeting note.

Many birds nest in cavities such as old woodpecker holes after the tenants have vacated them, natural tree cavities and man-made nesting boxes. Such boxes are utilized by bluebirds, purple martins, wrens, chickadees, titmice, nuthatches, house sparrows and starlings. It is legal to destroy the nests of house sparrows and starlings as these birds are not native to the United States. There are state and federal laws against destroying the nests of any other birds unless one has received a permit to take used nests from the site for teaching purposes.

EASTERN BLUEBIRD

Bulky nests are constructed by one of our smallest of birds, the wren. When nesting in a cavity, if they want a smaller entrance hole they plug part of it with sticks and thorns. Hummingbirds build the smallest of nests which are no larger than a halved English walnut. Nesting boxes are often used as places to snooze in the winter.

Most birds nest in trees, building their nests of sticks, twigs, grasses, feathers, and usually lining them with softer materials. I put out dryer lint and cotton for birds to use as a lining for their nests. One time I saw a robin taking the material from his old nest and moving it to another tree. Robins will also utilize nesting shelves which are built with a closed bottom, top, sides and back, but with the front open.

ROBIN'S NEST WITH EGGS

Nesting birds have many enemies. To keep wasps out of your nesting boxes, rub bar soap on the inside roof. If wasps have already started a nest there, open the box at night, remove the nest and then apply the soap. Predator guards can be placed on the entrance hole to keep cats, possums and other animals from being able to reach the eggs or babies. Also, a box can be mounted on a post or pole with a baffle beneath it. Grease can be painted on a mounting support to prevent snakes from slithering up to the nest box. Adding red pepper to the grease will force the snakes to eat more mice and rats and fewer baby birds. Grease will also keep ants out of the box.

House sparrows often destroy the eggs and babies of other cavity-nesting birds and will sometimes even kill the adults. In some areas, fence mounting is a stepladder for hungry night prowlers like cats, possums and raccoons. A flying squirrel will dine on bird eggs and may even take over the nesting box for its own.

I read an article recently entitled "Buzzards: The good, bad and ugly". The author said that buzzards (vultures) run the gauntlet from good to bad to ugly. I'll agree that they won't win any beauty contests, but they do a great job in cleaning up road kill and other animal carcasses. We'd live in a stinky world without vultures.

As for the bad, they sometimes take over deer stands for nesting sites. When the hunter climbs up his stand in the fall, he is greeted by a terrible odor and mess. This reminds me of a time when one of my sons found barn owls occupying three of his deer stands. After enclosing his stands to keep the owls out, he constructed a nesting box for them beneath a stand. It was used one year, but the owls have never returned to it since then.

I'll end this chapter with information about falconry, which is one of the world's most ancient forms of hunting. A falconer puts on a heavy leather glove that extends up the arm on which the hawk will perch. A falconer either buys or traps a wild hawk and trains it to be a hunter. The hawk needs to be hungry when it is taken out in the field to hunt. The falconer carries a long stick to beat the brush in order to flush out a rabbit or some other small animal for the hawk to grab. The bird has switched roles and is now the hunter, not the prey that birds usually are. One must take extensive training and get licensed before engaging in falconry.

SOME SPECIES NOT ALWAYS WELCOME

I will cover four animals in this chapter. I compare the good and bad qualities of three of them but cannot find anything good to say about feral hogs. They have been listed among the 100 most invasive and destructive animals in the world. A report in 2007 stated that North America had a population of five million feral hogs that cost Americans $1.5 billion annually in damage and efforts to eliminate them.

FERAL HOGS BY DEER STAND

The most damage is done by rooting for food and consumption of plant and animal matter grown for a food source for humans. The rooting causes erosion problems and destroys the plants being grown which may then be replaced by invasive species. The hogs also destroy deer stands, fences, nests of ground-nesting birds, and contaminate water supplies. Wild hogs also transmit diseases to domestic livestock.

Hog-vehicle wrecks result in a cost of an estimated $36 million in the United States each year. Such collisions often cause death to both drivers and the hogs. Too bad it's not just the pigs that fail to survive. The most popular methods of lethal control that are legal in the United States are trapping and then killing the pigs, ground shooting and aerial gunning.

Beavers are the largest North American rodents, some weighing as much as 50 pounds. They have dense brown fur and a black flattened scaly tail. They are often trapped for their valuable fur. So many had been destroyed by trapping that in 1900 they were almost extinct in some eastern states. As the price for the fur decreased, less trapping was done and the beaver populations increased.

BEAVER

Beavers build lodges in waterways, using tree limbs and logs and plaster them with mud and debris. These animals have extremely sharp teeth which makes it possible for them to gnaw down large wooden objects. One lodge was estimated to be 300 feet in length and over six feet high. Each lodge has a single entrance which is above the water tunneled down to their secluded areas. The good about beavers is due to the value of their fur; the bad is they often destroy desirable trees. Some people enclose the lower trunks of trees with chicken wire or tin to keep beavers from gnawing them down for their lodges.

Raccoons are small animals that resemble bears in structure. They have long, soft, thick fur that is sold for a fairly high price. Their heads and bodies are 22 to 26 inches in length and their tails are about 10 inches long. They are nocturnal and spend the daytime in trees. They nest in hollow trees. Their diet is mostly mice, frogs, crayfish, oysters, eggs and young birds. They often invade hen houses to feed on eggs there and sometimes chicks. In the summer they also eat fruits, depriving us of those peaches we looked forward to enjoying in a cobbler.

Raccoons usually live near water as they like to wash their food before ingesting it. This is the only animal I know that follows such a human-like practice. Raccoons may be more fastidious than some children that have to be asked before a meal, "Did you wash your hands?"

POSSUM

Possums are the only native North American marsupial. Their young can cling to their mothers back even as she climbs up a tall tree. Their fur is sold to make women's coats and used for trim on other garments. They eat fruits, mice, insects, frogs, eggs, and small birds. They also eat carrion. This, plus the value of their fur, are their two good traits. Ever hear the saying, "Possum in a 'simmon tree, raccoon on the ground?"

Although some species are not always welcome, Hersey's wise owl sitting in the oak and Aesop's sly fox hungering for the grapes are just two of the myriad things of the natural world that are welcomed to amaze us. God, through Mother Nature, has provided us with so much to enjoy. It is man's duty to preserve an environment that supports nature for generations to come. That way, young children of the future may continue to exclaim "Didn't Him do a good job!"

PHOTOGRAPH CREDITS
(Things for which no credit is listed were supplied by the author)